To see a World in a Grain of Sand
And Heaven in a Wild Flower
Hold Infinity in the palm of your hand
And Eternity in an hour

William Blake

Wild Flowers

An Easy Guide
by Habitat and Colour

Tracy Dickinson

Photos by Andrew N. Gagg

Green Books

First published in 2003
by Green Books Ltd
Foxhole, Dartington
Totnes, Devon TQ9 6EB
www.greenbooks.co.uk

Text © Tracy Dickinson 2003
Photographs © Andrew N. Gagg 2003
a.n.gagg@ntlworld.com

Book & cover design by Rick Lawrence
samskara@onetel.net.uk

Printed in Slovenia

British Library Cataloguing in Publication Data
available on request

ISBN 1 903998 20 4

Contents

Acknowledgements

Special thanks go out to my friends and family: their support and encouragement has played an integral part in the completion of this guide.

Thanks also to Andrew Gagg, Tim Jenkins of Farnborough College and other interested parties who have advised and commented on the structure and content of this guide. Finally, I would like to thank Green Books for publishing this book and turning a dream into a reality.

Introduction

This guide has been designed so that the most common wild flowers (both native and alien species) that are found throughout Britain can be quickly and easily identified by anybody, especially those with little or no botanical knowledge. People have used wild flowers over the centuries for a variety of purposes, including for flavouring foods and for their healing properties. Wild flowers are also displayed for their beauty in floral tributes and as a way to express emotions—such as sadness and sorrow at funerals, love and happiness at weddings, and on other special occasions.

The native wild flower population in Great Britain has changed dramatically over the centuries. As people have increasingly travelled the world, new species have been imported (both intentionally and accidentally), and have become native to this country.

Since the First World War, the distribution and numbers of flowers we see around Britain has dramatically changed. This is due to the increasing use of intensive agriculture, the greater use of herbicides, and the fragmentation and development of land in order to accommodate the increased population of Britain. Some species have become extinct, whilst many others have established themselves in the urban landscapes that we have created.

Charities and organisations such as The Wild Plant Conservation Society (Plantlife: www.plantlife.org.uk) and the Botanical Society of the British Isles (BSBI: www.bsbi.org.uk) have been formed with the purpose of protecting and conserving the existing wild flower populations of Britain through research, botanical surveys and public involvement.

In 1981 the Wildlife and Countryside Act made it illegal to uproot any wild flower without first gaining the permission of the landowner. It is strongly advised that any wild flowers that you see should **not** be picked or disturbed, but allowed to remain in their habit to be enjoyed by others.

Tracy Dickinson
February 2003

How to Use this Book

This guide has been designed to enable the user to identify a common wild flower in three easy steps, which are described below.

Step 1   On finding a wild flower, go to the habitat section in the book that best describes the area in which you have found the flower. There are eight habitats to choose from:

> Seashore & Coastal
> Fresh Water Habitats
> Marshes, Fens & Bogs
> Heaths & Moors
> Grassland & Meadows
> Arable & Waste Land
> Gardens, Paths & Walls
> Woodland & Hedgerows

Step 2   Once you have turned to the section of the book that best describes the area in which the flower has been found, there are introductory pages which display pictures of the common flowers you may find in that particular habitat. These pictures are grouped by colour to make it easier for you to scan quickly.

Step 3   From the section's introductory pages, pick the flower which best resembles the one you have seen. Then go to the corresponding page number that is displayed under the picture. The page will show a larger picture of the flower, along with a brief description and information that will help you to tell whether you have chosen the correct flower.

Names of wild flowers have changed through the ages and can also differ from region to region, in some cases there can be more than 100 different names for a single species of flower. In order to standardise the names in this guide, we have used the English names stated in *English Names of Wild Flowers* by Dony, Jury and Perring.

Seashore & Coastal

Sea Campion
14

Common
Scurvygrass 14

Sea-kale
14

Fairy Flax
15

Sea Mayweed
15

Prickly Saltwort
15

Sea Sandwort
16

Sea Beet
16

Common
Glasswort 16

Beaked
Tasselweed 17

Common
Twayblade 17

Wood Sage
17

Biting
Stonecrop 18

Yellow Horned-
poppy 18

Gorse
18

Black Medick
19

Common Bird's-
foot-trefoil 19

Kidney Vetch
19

Rock Samphire
20

Lady's Bedstraw
20

Common
Ragwort 20

Cat's-ear
21

Lesser Hawkbit
21

Henbane
21

Common
Restharrow 22

Dove's-foot
Crane's-bill 22

Common
Centaury 22

Herb-robert
23

Thrift
23

Sea Rocket
23

Sea Bindweed
24

Wild Thyme
24

Wild Onion
24

Tree-mallow
25

Sea Pea
25

Bittersweet
25

**Common
Sea-lavender** 26

Spring Squill
26

Harebell
26

Sea-holly
27

**Field Forget-
me-not** 27

Sea Aster
27

**Scarlet
Pimpernel** 28

Sea Campion
🏵 June–Aug
(Silene maritima) Campion Family

- Forked flowering stems grow to 30cm tall
- Scented white flowers have five overlapping petals that are deeply cut to more than half way down
- Spear-shaped; fleshy; waxy leaves are in opposite pairs up the stem
- Fruits are round capsules held within the flower parts • Insect-pollinated

Sea Campion is a hairless perennial of cliffs and shingle beaches around the coasts of Britain; sometimes mistaken for Bladder Campion.

Common Scurvygrass
🏵 May–Aug
(Cochlearia officinalis) Cabbage Family

- Flowering stems up to 50cm tall
- White flowers have four petals loosely clustered on short stalks towards the top of the stem
- Leaves at the bottom of the plant are on long stalks and mostly heart-shaped; stem leaves are smaller, triangular and clasping the stem
- Fruits are round capsules • Insect-pollinated

A hairless biennial or perennial of cliffs and salt-marshes throughout Britain, although very rare in the south and south-east. Rich in vitamin C.

Sea-kale
🏵 May–Aug
(Crambe maritime) Cabbage Family

- Stems grow up to 60cm tall
- White flowers have four petals and are gathered in flat branched clusters
- Leaves at base of plant are large, waxy, stalked and lobed with wavy margins. Stem leaves are smaller and stalkless.
- Fruits are one-seeded and spherical
- Insect-pollinated

A perennial of undisturbed shingle beaches and sandy shores throughout most of Britain, but absent from the far northern coasts. The young shoots can be eaten as a vegetable.

Fairy Flax   ❀ June–Sept
(Linum catharticum) Flax Family

- Slender forked flowering stems up to 15cm tall
- White flowers with five petals are in loose nodding clusters
- Leaves are blunt, oval-oblong, stalkless and in opposite pairs up the delicate stems
- Fruits are round capsules
- Insect-pollinated

A delicate annual of cliff-tops, sand dunes, and grasslands, preferring limestone and chalk soils. Another common name is Purging Flax, probably due to its past use as a purgative.

Sea Mayweed   ❀ July–Sept
(Tripleurospermum maritimum) Daisy Family

- Hairless branched stems up to 50cm tall
- Flowers have an outer ray of white florets with a central disc of short yellow florets, flowers are up to 4cm across and held in loose clusters.
- Alternate leaves are divided up to three times with each segment divided again into very narrow, almost thread-like parts.

A scentless annual herb of cultivated and arable land, wasteland and roadside verges throughout Britain.

Prickly Saltwort   ❀ July–Sept
(Salsola kali) Goosefoot Family

- Grows to 40cm tall
- Flowers are tiny and white, forming where the leaves meet the stems
- Leaves are small, fleshy with a spine at the tip

Prickly Saltwort is a succulent annual, commonly found on the drift line of sandy beaches around the coast of Britain. The juice of this plant has been used as a diuretic.

Sea Sandwort   ❀ May–Aug
(Honkenya peploides) Campion Family

- Stems up to 15cm tall
- Small flowers are greenish-white and few in number, in loose clusters on branched stems
- Yellowish-green to green leaves are small, oval-pointed and fleshy
- Fruits are round yellowish green capsules
- Self-pollinated

Sea Sandwort is a fleshy creeping perennial of shingle beaches and sand dunes around the coast of Britain.

Sea Beet   ❀ July–Sept
(Beta vulgaris) Goose-foot Family

- Stems up to 100cm tall
- Tiny green flowers are gathered in densely clustered spikes
- Leaves are stalked, dark green, triangular and glossy
- Wind-pollinated

Sea Beet is a fleshy perennial found around the coasts of Britain on sand dunes, shingle beaches, cliffs and sea walls. This plant can also be found inland on salt marshes.

Common Glasswort   ❀ Aug–Sept
(Salicornia europaea) Glasswort Family

- Grows to 30cm tall
- Minute green flowers are grouped in threes and have one or two yellow stamens
- Leaves are tiny green lobes that are indistinguishable from the swollen, fleshy, segmented stems
- Fruits are small nutlets, released from the stem

Common Glasswort, also known as Marsh Samphire, is a low-growing annual with opposite fleshy branches off a main stem. It grows in saltmarshes around the coast of Britain.

Beaked Tasselweed
🌸 July–Sept
(Ruppia maritima) Tasselweed Family

- Branched stems grow to 40cm long
- Flowers are small, green, without petals and are gathered in small stalked clusters
- Submerged leaves are long, alternate or opposite, narrow and grass-like
- Fruits are stalked clusters of nutlets

Beaked Tasselweed is an aquatic perennial of salt marshes, saltwater pools and ditches around the coasts of Britain.

Common Twayblade
🌸 May–July
(Listera ovata) Orchid Family

- Grows up to 60cm tall
- Green to yellowish-green flowers have no spurs and are gathered in long spikes
- Leaves are an opposite pair of broad, oval and ribbed leaves towards the base of the stem
- Fruits are twisted capsules
- Insect-pollinated

Common Twayblade is a perennial herb of rough grasslands, open woodlands, scrub and heaths throughout most of Britain, although quite rare in the higher regions of Scotland.

Wood Sage
🌸 June–Sept
(Teucrium scorodonia) Mint Family

- Grows to 60cm tall
- Yellowish-green flowers with only a lower lobed lip are in opposite pairs and grouped in branched spikes
- Toothed leaves have a wrinkled surface, are heart-shaped at the base and in opposite pairs up the stem
- Fruits are nutlets • Insect-pollinated

A downy perennial herb with square stems that are often flushed red. It is a flower of open woodlands, sand dunes, rough grasslands and heaths.

Biting Stonecrop   ❀ June–Aug
(Sedum acre) Stonecrop Family

- Stems grow to 10cm tall
- Bright yellow flowers are star-shaped with five petals, much larger than the leaves
- Leaves are tiny; oval, fleshy and overlapping
- Fruits are pods
- Pollinated by bees

A hairless perennial of dry coastal areas such as shingle beaches and sand dunes, as well as on walls and rocky ground. The shoots have a distinctly peppery taste, which has led to the flower's other common name of Wall-pepper.

Yellow Horned-poppy   ❀ June–Sept
(Glaucium flavum) Poppy Family

- Branched flowering stems grow to 100cm tall
- Large (up to 9cm across) solitary flowers are yellow with four flimsy petals
- Waxy leaves are greyish-green and slightly hairy. Long root leaves are deeply cut into slightly toothed lobes; stem leaves are shorter, less divided and clasp the stem
- Insect-pollinated • Fruits are long curved pods

A greyish-green perennial of shingle beaches around the coasts of Britain although fairly rare in the south-west of Scotland. When the stems are cut, this flower bleeds a poisonous yellow sap.

Gorse   ❀ mainly April–Oct
(Ulex europaeus) Pea Family

- Stems up to 300cm tall
- Scented yellow flowers are in clusters towards the end of spiny branches
- Young shrubs have leaves that are small and divided into three leaflets. Older shrubs develop sharp branched spines
- Fruits are hairy, black, flattish pods
- Insect-pollinated

Gorse is an evergreen spiny shrub of sea cliffs, heathland, open woodlands and wasteland. The seeds of this plant can lay dormant in the ground for many years before germinating.

Black Medick
(Medicago lupulina) Pea Family

✿ April–Aug

- Stems up to 60cm long
- Tiny yellow flowers are clustered together forming small rounded heads
- Leaves are short-stalked and divided into three oval leaflets, each leaflet slightly notched
- Fruits are clusters of tiny kidney-shaped pods on long stalks, and turn black when ripe
- Self-pollinated

A hairy annual or short-lived perennial of grasslands, roadsides, shingle beaches, coastal cliffs and sand dunes of Britain. Can be distinguished from yellow clovers by its black fruits.

Common Bird's-foot-trefoil
(Lotus corniculatus) Pea Family

✿ June–Sept

- Grows up to 40cm tall
- Golden yellow flowers are two-lipped and sometimes flushed red or orange. Up to eight flowers are gathered at the top of a long stalk
- Leaves are divided into five pointed-oval leaflets
- Fruits are long pods that are arranged like a 'bird's foot' • Insect-pollinated

Bird's-foot Trefoil is a perennial of short grasslands, roadsides, cliffs and coastal areas of Britain. Has many local names such as 'bacon and eggs' and 'ham and eggs'.

Kidney Vetch
(Anthyllis vulneraria) Pea Family

✿ June–Sept

- Grows up to 30cm tall
- Tiny yellow flowers are clustered in paired rounded heads with a ruff of small leaf-like bracts below. White and woolly at base of flowers
- Leaves are divided into opposite pairs of oval-pointed leaflets with an end leaflet. The green leaves are silvery and hairy underneath
- Fruits are one-seeded flat oval pods held in the flower parts

A soft, hairy perennial of dry grasslands, sand dunes and cliffs, preferring chalky or limestone soils. Can be found in a variety of other colours.

Rock Samphire
※ June–Aug

(Crithmum maritimum) Carrot Family

- Ridged, solid stems grow to 30cm tall
- Tiny yellow flowers are grouped in flat-topped umbels
- Pale bluish-green leaves on short stalks are divided 2–3 times into fleshy narrow segments
- Fruits are ridged, egg-shaped capsules

A hairless perennial of coastal rocks, cliffs and shingle beaches around Britain, though mainly found on the south and west coasts. This fleshy plant is edible and has been harvested in the past for cooking or pickling.

Lady's Bedstraw
※ July–Sept

(Galium verum) Bedstraw Family

- Square stems grow to 80cm tall
- Scented yellow flowers are tiny with four petals and are clustered along the branched stems
- Leaves are narrow and in whorls of up to twelve around the stem • Insect-pollinated

A perennial herb with creeping stems, growing on sand dunes, coastal heaths and on some grasslands and hedge banks. In the past this flower was commonly used as a stuffing for mattresses and as a flea deterrent.

Common Ragwort
※ June–Nov

(Senecio jacobaea) Daisy Family

- Grows up to 150cm tall
- Daisy-like flowers are yellow and gathered in branched, flattish-topped clusters
- Leaves are dark green, deeply lobed and slightly toothed. Upper leaves clasp the stem
- Fruits are one-seeded with a top of white hairs
- Insect-pollinated

Ragwort is a biennial or on occasion perennial of rough grasslands, wasteland, roadsides and sand dunes. This plant is toxic to livestock and is therefore pulled extensively in the summer by landowners and conservation groups.

Cat's-ear
❀ June–Sept

(Hypochoeris radicata) Daisy Family

- Smooth, few-branching stems grow to 40cm
- Flowers are solitary on stems, with rays of strap-shaped florets. Outer florets greyish underneath
- Toothed leaves are hairy, gently lobed and arranged in a rosette around the stem base. Flowering stems have tiny scale-like leaves
- Fruits are one-seeded with white feathery hairs at the top • Insect-pollinated

A perennial herb of dunes, grasslands, meadows and roadsides. Dandelion-like, but has smaller flowers and less fleshy stems. Leaves are edible.

Lesser Hawkbit
❀ June–Sept

(Leontodon taraxacoides) Daisy Family

- Flowering stems up to 25cm tall
- Yellow flowers are solitary and droop when in bud. Petals are rays of strap-like florets with the outer florets greyish underneath
- Leaves are toothed, hairy, gently lobed and in a rosette around the stem base
- Fruits are one-seeded with white feathery hairs at the top • Insect- or wind-pollinated

A hairy perennial of sandy, well-drained soils of dry grasslands, roadsides, heaths and stable dunes.

Henbane
❀ June–Aug

(Hyoscyamus niger) Nightshade Family

- Hairy flowering stems grow up to 80cm tall
- Pale yellow five-lobed flowers with distinctive purple veins and centre, flowering in two rows up the stem
- Large leaves are oblong-oval, most being deeply toothed. Stem leaves are clasping and lower leaves stalked
- Fruits are round capsules opening at the top

Henbane is a very poisonous hairy annual or biennial of coastal sandy ground, wasteland and farmland. The leaves and stem of this plant have a distinctive smell.

Common Restharrow 🌸 June–Sept
(Ononis repens) Pea Family

- Round hairy stems up are to 80cm long and 30cm high
- Pink flowers are two-lipped, emerging from the leaf base
- Leaves are divided into three pointed, oval, toothed, hairy leaflets
- Fruits are pods that split to release the seeds

A perennial found on sand dunes and grassland around the coasts of Britain, although rarer in the north-west of Scotland. This plant has roots that are said to taste of liquorice.

Dove's-foot Crane's-bill 🌸 April–Sept
(Geranium molle) Geranium Family

- Branched hairy stems grow to 10cm tall
- Pink flowers have five notched petals
- Leaves are rounded and cut into 5–7 toothed lobes
- Fruits are hairless, pointed capsules
- Self-pollinated

Dove's-foot Crane's-bill is an annual of dry grassland, sand dunes, wasteland, cultivated and arable land. This plant is similar to other crane's-bills, especially the Small-flowered Crane's-bill, but has smaller hairs on the stems.

Common Centaury 🌸 June–Oct
(Centaurium erythraea) Gentian Family

- Square stems up to 50cm tall
- Pink tubular flowers with five spreading petals, grouped together on top of branched stems
- Pale green leaves at base are oval-oblong in a rosette; stem leaves are pointed-oval in opposite pairs
- Fruits are many-seeded capsules
- Self- or insect-pollinated

An annual of sand dunes, cliffs, woodland margins and grasslands around the coast of Britain. It is the most common flower of the Gentian family and has been used in the past to aid digestion.

Herb-robert
❀ May–Sept

(Geranium robertianum) Gentian Family

- Flushed hairy stems grow to 50cm tall
- Pink flowers have five petals with pale streaks on paired branches off the stem
- Bright green leaves are divided into deeply cut leaflets
- Fruits are beak-like capsules

Herb-robert is a strong-smelling, hairy annual herb of woodlands, hedgerows, shaded gardens and shingle beaches of Britain. It can be mistaken for another flower, Little-Robin, although this has smaller flowers and yellow anthers.

Thrift
❀ April–Oct

(Armeria maritima) Sea-lavender Family

- Grows to 30cm tall
- Scented pink flowers have five petals and are closely grouped together to form rounded heads
- Grass-like leaves grow from the base of the plant
- Fruits are one-seeded capsules
- Insect-pollinated

Thrift is a mat-forming perennial of cliffs, rocks and salt marshes around the coast of Britain. This flower, also known as Sea Pink, can also be found further inland on mountain ledges.

Sea Rocket
❀ June–Sept

(Cakile maritime) Cabbage Family

- Pink-lilac flowers have four petals clustered on short stalks towards the top of the stems
- Bluish to greyish-green leaves are fleshy, stalked and deeply lobed
- Fruits are short pointed-oval capsules on thick stalks
- Insect-pollinated

Sea Rocket is a hairless annual herb found on sandy coasts, and is one of the first flowers to colonise young dunes.

Sea Bindweed   ❀ June–Aug
(Calystegia soldanella) Bindweed Family

- Creeping hairless stems to 50cm long
- Pink flowers are trumpet-shaped with white stripes
- Stalked leaves are fleshy, dark green and kidney-shaped
- Fruits are small capsules
- Self- or insect-pollinated

Sea Bindweed is a hairless, creeping perennial found on sandy beaches around the coasts of Britain. The leaf-like bracts of this flower open in sunlight and close at night.

Wild Thyme   ❀ May–Aug
(Thymus polytrichus) Mint Family

- Square hairy stems grow to 10cm tall
- Tiny pink to purplish-pink flowers are two-lipped and grouped together in round spikes
- Leaves are spear-shaped and in opposite pairs up the stem
- Fruits are four nutlets held within the remaining flower parts • Insect-pollinated

An aromatic perennial herb found in short chalk grassland, coastal heaths, rocks, and sand dunes of Britain. It is a mat-forming plant with a distinctive smell and hairs only on two opposite sides of the square stem.

Wild Onion   ❀ June–July
(Allium vineale) Lily Family

- Grows to 80cm tall
- Pink to purplish-pink flowers grow on stalks from a rounded head of purplish-green, oval bulbs that are partly covered by a paper spathe. The flowers of this plant are not always present
- Long narrow leaves are almost tubular
- Insect-pollinated

A hairless perennial of fixed dunes, arable land, hedgebanks, dry grasslands and roadsides. This plant is also known as Crow Garlic, as it smells strongly of garlic when bruised.

Tree-mallow ❀ July–Sept
(Lavatera arborea) Mallow Family

- Woody stems up to 300cm tall
- Purplish-pink flowers with a dark purple centre and five petals with purple veins are grouped together in a flowering spike
- Large downy leaves are stalked, with 5–7 triangular-shaped lobes
- Fruits are one-seeded, held within the flower parts

Tree-mallow is a woody tree-like biennial of wasteland and cliffs and rocky areas around the coasts of southern and eastern Britain.

Sea Pea ❀ May–Sept
(Lathyrus japonicus) Pea Family

- Square stems up to 100cm long
- Two-lipped purple flowers turning bluish. Flowers in loose, stalked clusters of up to 15 towards top of stem
- Leaves divided into pairs of greyish-green, oval leaflets. End leaflet usually ends in a tendril
- Fruits are pods that split when ripe
- Insect-pollinated, mainly by bees

A hairless perennial herb found predominantly on the shingle beaches of the southern and eastern shores of Britain. The peas in the pods can be cooked and eaten like those of the garden pea.

Bittersweet ❀ June–Sept
(Solanum dulcamara) Nightshade Family

- Scrambling woody stems grow to 200cm tall
- Loose branched purple flowers with five turned-back petals and a cone-shaped cluster of yellow stamens
- Leaves are stalked, pointed-oval, some with two opposite leaflets at the base. Stem leaves are narrower
- Fruits are drooping clusters of bright red oval berries

Bittersweet is a hairy perennial of shingle beaches, woodlands, hedge banks and damp shady areas. The whole of this plant is poisonous.

SEASHORE & COASTAL

Common Sea-lavender ❀ July–Oct
(Limonium vulgare) Sea-lavender Family

- Branched leafless stems grow to 50cm tall
- Small purplish-blue flowers in flat-topped branched clusters
- Spoon-shaped leaves are in a rosette around the base of the plant
- Fruits are single-seeded capsules
- Insect-pollinated

Common Sea-lavender is a perennial of salt-marshes across Britain.

Spring Squill ❀ April–June
(Scilla verna) Lily Family

- Leafless stalks grow up to 15cm tall
- Star-like violet-blue flowers have six petals and are loosely clustered at the top of the stem. Each flower has a purplish-blue bract
- Leaves are long, grass-like and curly
- Fruits are capsules
- Insect-pollinated

Spring Squill is a hairless perennial growing on short grassland along the west coast of Britain.

Harebell ❀ July–Oct
(Campanula rotundifolia) Bellflower Family

- Slender flowering stems grow to 40cm tall
- Blue, nodding bell-shaped flowers
- Leaves at base of flower are toothed, long stalked and rounded with a heart-shaped base; stem leaves are narrow, short stalked or stalkless and less toothed.
- Fruits are rounded capsules
- Self- or insect-pollinated

A delicate-looking hairless perennial of fixed sand dunes, dry grasslands, hedgerows and heaths throughout Britain.

Sea-holly ❀ July–Sept
(Eryngium maritimum) Carrot Family

- Grows up to 60cm tall
- Tiny flowers are clustered together in rounded heads. Below each head of flowers is a whorl of leaf-like spiny bracts
- Toothed leaves are rounded and have spiny tips on the end of each tooth. Leaves are bluish- to greyish-green with white veins
- Tiny fruits are covered in hooked bristles

Sea-holly is a distinctive branched perennial of sandy beaches and shingle beaches around the coast of Britain.

Field Forget-me-not ❀ April–Sept
(Myosotis arvensis) Borage Family

- Hairy flowering stems grow to 40cm tall
- Pale blue flowers have five petals and a yellow central eye
- Leaves are hairy and mainly stalkless, with one central vein
- Fruits are nutlets which are held within the remaining flower parts

Field Forget-me-not (or Common Forget-me-not) is a hairy annual of disturbed ground, cultivated and arable land, roadsides and some waste ground.

Sea Aster ❀ July–Oct
(Aster tripolium) Daisy Family

- Grows up to 100cm tall
- Daisy-like flowers with central yellow disc surrounded by a ray of mauve florets in loose branched clusters
- Alternate leaves are narrow, spear-shaped with one central vein
- Fruits are one-seeded with white hairs at the top
- Insect-pollinated

Sea Aster is a short-lived perennial that grows around the coasts of Britain on cliffs, rocks and salt marshes.

Scarlet Pimpernel
✿ June–Aug

(Anagallis arvensis) Primrose Family

- Angled stems grow to around 40cm long
- Small scarlet flowers are dish-shaped and have five lobes. Flowers are solitary on long slender stalks, which arise in pairs from where the leaves meet the stem
- Leaves are oval, pointed with black dots on the underside and are in opposite pairs
- Fruits are capsules

An annual weed of open grassland, sand dunes and cultivated and arable land, preferring well-drained soils.

Fresh Water Habitats

Common Water-starwort 34

Perfoliate Pondweed 34

Broad-leaved Pondweed 34

Common Nettle 35

Mare's-tail 35

Marsh Pennywort 35

Wild Angelica 36

Common Valerian 36

Butterbur 36

Winter Heliotrope 37

Amphibious Bistort 37

Redshank 37

Great Willow-herb 38

Marsh Woundwort 38

Indian Balsam 38

Purple-loosestrife 39

Spiked Water-milfoil 39

Hemlock Water-dropwort 39

Hemlock 40

Water-cress 40

Fool's Water-cress 40

Gipsywort 41

White Water-lily 41

Common Comfrey 41

Pond Water-crowfoot 42

Water-plantain 42

Branched Bur-reed 42

Wood Bitter-cress 43

Celery-leaved Buttercup 43

Opposite-leaved G.-saxifrage 43

Colt's-foot 44

Yellow Iris 44

Tansy
44

Greater Bladderwort 45

Monkey Flower
45

Yellow Loosestrife 45

Lesser Spearwort 46

Water Forget-me-not 46

Water Mint
46

Skullcap
47

Brooklime
47

Bulrush
47

Montbretia
48

Common Water-starwort ❀ May–Sept
(Callitriche stagnalis)
Water Starwort Family

- Grows to 100cm long
- Flowers are minute and green
- Oval leaves are blunt and in opposite pairs; rosettes of leaves can be seen at the water surface
- Fruits are tiny and winged • Wind-pollinated

A hairless annual or perennial herb of ponds, streams, ditches and some wet areas of woodlands. It is the most common of the Water-starwort species, but it is very difficult to distinguish between them.

Perfoliate Pondweed ❀ May–Sept
(Potamogeton perfoliatus)
Pondweed Family

- Submerged stems grow to 300cm long
- Tiny green flowers are gathered in dense spikes emerging from the water
- Translucent green leaves are stalkless, oval and totally submerged under the water
- Fruits are green nutlets

Perfoliate Pondweed is an almost totally submerged aquatic plant of still and slow moving water.

Broad-leaved Pondweed ❀ May–Sept
(Potamogeton natans) Pondweed Family

- Submerged stems grow to 300cm long
- Tiny green flowers are gathered in dense spikes emerging from the water
- Large leathery submerged and floating leaves are pointed oblong to oval on long stalks
- Fruits are small green nutlets

Broad-leaved Pondweed is a submerged aquatic plant of still and slow moving water. Pondweeds are usually hard to distinguish from one another, but the large dark green leaves of this plant are distinctive.

Common Nettle   ❀ June–Aug
(Urtica dioica) Nettle Family

- Hairy stems grow to 150cm tall
- Tiny green flowers without petals are grouped together in drooping clusters emerging from the base of the leaf stalks
- Stalked leaves are toothed, pointed with a heart-shaped base
- Wind-pollinated

A hairy perennial that grows well in many habitats such as wasteland, woodlands, hedge banks, roadsides and fens, and by rivers and streams. Both the stem and leaves are covered in stinging hairs that irritate the skin on contact.

Mare's-tail   ❀ June–July
(Hippuris vulgaris) Mare's-tail Family

- Grows to 70cm tall
- Tiny green flowers are without petals and often unnoticeable
- Small, narrow leaves are in many whorls around the stem
- Wind-pollinated

Mare's-tail is a perennial aquatic herb with erect unbranched stems. It is a plant of still and slow moving freshwater habitats. The whorls of short, narrow leaves make this plant distinctive.

Marsh Pennywort   ❀ June–Aug
(Hydrocotyle vulgaris) Carrot Family

- Leaf stalks grow up to 20cm tall
- Minute pinkish-green flowers are stalkless and in whorls around the stem
- Round leaves are on long stalks and slightly toothed
- Fruits are tiny round, flattish capsules
- Self-pollinated

Marsh Pennywort is a creeping perennial of bogs and marshes, also found by streams and other wet areas.

Wild Angelica ❀ June–Sept
(Angelica sylvestris) Carrot Family

- Grooved stems are flushed purple and grow to 200cm tall
- Minute pink or white flowers are gathered in stalked clusters forming dome-shaped heads up to 15cm across
- Leaves are divided into 2–3 pairs of pointed, oval and toothed leaflets, with an end leaflet. There are broad sheaths at the base of the stems

An erect hairless perennial found by streams, rivers, lakes, ditches, wet meadows, marshes and fens preferring more calcareous soils. Has been used to produce a yellow dye as well as a flavouring.

Common Valerian ❀ June–Aug
(Valeriana officinalis) Valerian Family

- Grooved stems grow to 120cm tall
- Small, scented, pinkish-white flowers with five petals are grouped together at the top of branched stems
- Opposite leaves are divided into pairs of toothed spear-shaped leaflets with a similar end leaflet. Lower stem leaves are stalked.
- Fruits are one-seeded with white hairs at the top
- Insect-pollinated

Common Valerian is a perennial of riversides, fens, marshes and damp woodlands. This plant has been used in the past as a sedative.

Butterbur ❀ March–May
(Petasites hybridus) Daisy Family

- Grows to 40cm tall
- Lilac-pink flowers are gathered in stalked spikes
- Leaves are large, toothed, heart-shaped and are on long stalks. The leaves of this plant appear after the flowers

Butterbur is a distinctive perennial with creeping underground stems. It is a plant of wet woodlands, roadsides and wet meadows, and is also found by streams and rivers. Its common name derives from the past use of its leaves to wrap butter.

Winter Heliotrope   ✿ Nov–March
(Petasites fragrans) Daisy Family

- Hairy stems grow up to 25cm tall
- Vanilla-scented, lilac flowers are bell-shaped with an outer ray of florets. Flowers are in a loose spike
- Large toothed leaves are stalked, rounded and kidney-shaped; stem leaves are small and scale-like
- Fruits are one-seeded with a top of white hairs
- Insect-pollinated

A perennial with creeping underground stems found on wasteland, hedge banks, roadsides and by rivers and streams.

Amphibious Bistort   ✿ July–Sept
(Polygonum amphibium) Dock Family

- Grows to 70cm long
- Tiny pink or reddish flowers are in dense cylindrical spikes at the end of the stems
- Alternate leaves are oblong or spear-shaped; floating leaves have heart-shaped bases
- Fruits are tiny, brown and lens-shaped

Amphibious Bistort is a perennial with flowering stems, and as the name suggests is a plant that grows well in or out of the water. It is found in wetland habitats: by lakes, ponds, rivers, ditches or marshes.

Redshank   ✿ June–Oct
(Polygonum persicaria) Dock Family

- Flushed red stems grow to 80cm tall
- Tiny pink flowers are tightly gathered in a cylindrical spike
- Leaves are alternate and spear-shaped
- Fruits are tiny, black and shiny
- Self- or insect-pollinated

Redshank, also known as Persicaria, is a hairless annual weed of arable and cultivated land, wasteland, and roadsides and by rivers and streams throughout Britain.

Great Willow-herb
❀ July–Aug
(Epilobium hirsutum) Willowherb Family

- Downy perennial growing to 150cm tall
- Purplish-pink flowers are held in loose branched clusters
- Shallowly toothed leaves are in opposite pairs and slightly clasping the stems
- Fruits are long slender capsules
- Self- or insect-pollinated

Grows on marshes, fens and by the sides of streams, rivers, ponds and ditches. The seeds that are contained within the capsules have white hairs attached to them that aid their dispersal by the wind.

Marsh Woundwort
❀ July–Sept
(Stachys palustris) Mint Family

- Square, hollow stems grow to 100cm tall
- Pinkish-purple flowers are two-lipped with white markings on lower lip and are in whorls around the stem above each pair of leaves
- Opposite pairs of toothed leaves are stalked on lower stem and stalkless above
- Fruits are nutlets that are held within the remaining flower parts • Pollinated by bees

A hairy perennial with creeping underground roots. It is a plant of marshes and freshwater margins throughout most of Britain, although quite scarce in some highland parts of Scotland.

Indian Balsam
❀ July–Oct
(Impatiens glandulifera) Balsam Family

- Flushed red stems grow to 250cm tall
- Pink to purplish-pink flowers are two-lipped with short spurs and are gathered in stalked, loose nodding clusters
- Red-toothed leaves are in whorls of three around the stem
- Fruits are green drooping capsules, which explode to release seeds when ripe
- Insect-pollinated

This annual of riversides, streamsides and other damp shady places was introduced to Britain in the early 19th Century. It has a distinctive scent.

Purple-loosestrife
✿ June–Aug

(Lythrum salicaria)
Purple-loosestrife Family

- Angled stems grow to 150cm tall
- Red-purple flowers (up to 1.5cm across) with six petals, grouped together in long spikes up to 30cm long
- Leaves are pointed-oval in opposite pairs or in threes. Leaves become smaller up the stem
- Fruits are oval capsules • Insect-pollinated

Purple-loosestrife is a downy perennial found in marshes and by the sides of rivers and streams throughout Britain, apart from the far north of Scotland.

Spiked Water-milfoil
✿ June–Aug

(Myriophyllum spicatum)
Water-milfoil Family

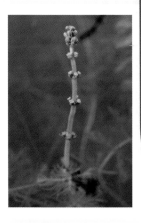

- Submerged branching stems grow to 200cm long
- Tiny red flowers in whorls around the stem above the water
- Leaves are mostly in whorls of four around the submerged stems. Each leaf is cut into many narrow strand-like segments • Wind-pollinated

An aquatic perennial herb of still and running freshwater habitats. The stems that emerge from the water are usually leafless and quite distinctive.

Hemlock Water-dropwort
✿ June–Sept

(Oenanthe crocata) Carrot Family

- Hairless, hollow stems up to 150cm tall
- Tiny white flowers clustered in dome-shaped heads up to 15cm across
- Leaf triangular overall and divided into 3–4 pairs of deeply wedged leaflets

Hemlock Water-dropwort is a hairless perennial that can be found throughout Britain (although rare to the east and in Scotland), by ditches, lakes, rivers and streams. The whole of this plant is very poisonous and has been used in the past as a rat poison.

Hemlock   ❀ June–July
(Conium maculatum) Carrot Family

- Grooved flowering stems with purple blotches grow to 200cm tall
- Tiny white flowers with five petals are gathered in flat-topped umbels
- Leaves growing to 40cm long are separated into deeply divided fern-like leaflets
- Rounded fruits, one-seeded with wavy ridges

A hairless, unpleasant-smelling biennial of roadside verges, damp wasteland and the sides of streams and rivers throughout Britain, although quite rare in parts of Scotland. The whole of this plant is poisonous and should not be touched.

Water-cress   ❀ May–Oct
(Rorippa nasturtium-aquaticum) Cabbage Family

- Grows up to 50cm tall
- Tiny white flowers have four petals and are loosely clustered at the top of each stem
- Dark green leaves are divided into pairs of oval to spear-shaped leaflets
- Fruits are pods containing two rows of seeds
- Insect-pollinated

Water-cress is a hairless perennial of ditches, streams and rivers throughout most of Britain. It is rich in vitamin C, and is cultivated for its culinary uses.

Fool's Water-cress   ❀ July–Aug
(Apium nodiflorum) Carrot Family

- Branched stems grow to 80cm tall
- Minute flowers are grouped to form umbels that arise from where the leaf meets the stem
- Leaves are divided into 4–6 pairs of shiny, toothed oval leaflets with a similar end leaflet

Fool's Water-cress is a hairless perennial of ponds, streams and ditches. This plant can be mistaken for Water-cress, especially as they grow in similar habitats, but they can be distinguished by their flowers.

Gipsywort
❀ June–Sept
(Lycopus europaeus) Mint Family

- Square stems grow to 100cm tall
- Small, white bell-shaped flowers have purple dots on the lower of the four lobes. Flowers are arranged in whorls around the stem at the base of each pair of leaves
- Spear-shaped leaves are deeply toothed and in opposite pairs along the stem
- Fruits are four individual nutlets held within the remaining flower parts • Insect-pollinated

Gipsywort is a hairy perennial herb that is found beside streams, rivers, ponds, ditches and some wet woodlands, favouring fertile and peaty soils.

White Water-lily
❀ July–Aug
(Nymphaea alba) Water-lily Family

- Underwater stems grow to 300cm long
- Large (to 20cm across) single white flower with many petals and a yellow centre
- Leathery, waxy leaves are circular with a deep wedge-shaped cut; leaves are floating and are on long underwater stems
- Fruits are round green capsules that sink below the surface when ripe
- Self- or insect-pollinated

White Water-lily is an aquatic perennial of still fresh water such as lakes and ponds. It is one of the largest wild flowers in Britain.

Common Comfrey
❀ May–June
(Symphytum officinale) Borage Family

- Grows up to 120cm tall
- White or pink flowers are tubular to narrowly bell-shaped and are gathered in loose drooping clusters at the end of branched stems
- Leaves at the base of the plant are stalked and broadly spear-shaped
- Stem leaves are smaller, narrower and can be in wing-like pairs
- Fruits are shiny black nutlets • Insect-pollinated

A perennial flower growing beside, rivers, streams, marshes and ditches. Very nutrient-rich; seen in many allotments, where it is used as compost.

FRESH WATER HABITATS

Pond Water-crowfoot ❀ May–Sept
(Ranunculus peltatus) Buttercup Family

- Flowers are white with yellow colouring towards the base of the five petals, and are held on stalks off the main stem
- Leaves are kidney-shaped in outline but divided into three or more lobes, toothed at the ends.

Common Water-crowfoot is a characteristic plant of still and running water, including ponds, lakes and shallow streams. This plant is quite rare in some parts of Scotland.

FRESH WATER HABITATS

Water-plantain ❀ June–Aug
(Alisma plantago-aquatica)
Water-plantain Family

- Grows up to 100cm tall
- White flowers have three petals and a yellow centre. Flowers are on slender stalks that are in whorls around the branched stems
- Leaves are pointed; oval, long-stalked and basal
- Fruits are one-seeded and flattish
- Insect-pollinated

This hairless perennial is a characteristic plant of fresh water habitats such as streams, rivers, ditches and ponds. Found throughout Britain but quite rare in some parts of Scotland.

Branched Bur-reed ❀ June–Aug
(Sparganium erectum) Bur-reed family

- Branched stems grow up to 150cm tall
- Minute white flowers are grouped together to form spiky-looking ball-shaped clusters
- Leaves are grass-like and slightly folded in from the centre
- Fruit is a nutlet contained within a rounded spiky head
- Wind-pollinated

Branched Bur-reed is a hairless perennial growing throughout Britain in the shallow waters of lakes, rivers, ponds and canals. Rare in the far north of Scotland.

Wood Bitter-cress ❀ March–Sept
(Cardamine flexuosa) Cabbage Family

- Wavy stems grow to 35cm tall
- Tiny white flowers have four petals and are gathered in short-stalked clusters
- Leaves are divided into opposite pairs of rounded, slightly toothed or untoothed leaflets. All leaves have a similar end leaflet Stem leaves are smaller with narrower leaflets
- Fruits are long, narrow pods

Wood Bitter-cress is a perennial of woodland flushes, wasteland and gardens, preferring damp shady areas.

Celery-leaved Buttercup ❀ May–Sept
(Ranunculus sceleratus) Buttercup Family

- Hollow branched stems grow to 60cm tall
- Small flowers have five shiny, pale yellow petals
- Leaves are pale green and shiny. Leaves at the bottom of the plant are on long stalks and divided into three broad, deeply toothed lobes. Stem leaves are narrower and less toothed
- Fruits are nutlets contained in rounded heads
- Insect-pollinated

A hairless annual found on the muddy verges of lakes, rivers and ponds as well as wet meadows. The whole of this plant is poisonous, with a sap that can blister the skin.

Opposite-leaved Golden-saxifrage ❀ April–July
(Chrysosplenium oppositifolium) Saxifrage Family

- Perennial herb growing to 15cm tall
- Tiny yellow flowers are without petals, and are surrounded by yellowish-green leaf-like structures (bracts)
- Opposite pairs of leaves are rounded, bluntly toothed with a wedge-shaped base
- Fruits are tiny capsules • Self- or insect-pollinated

A plant of wet woodlands, stream sides and wet rocks. Alternate-leaved Golden-saxifrage looks similar but has alternate, kidney-shaped leaves.

Colt's-foot ❀ Feb–April
(Tussilago farfara) Daisy Family

- Scaly flowering stems grow to 30cm tall
- Solitary flowers are yellow and consist of disc florets and an outer ray of many narrow florets
- Large stalked leaves are heart-shaped and toothed with silvery-white hairs below
- Fruits are nutlets with a top of white hairs
- Insect-pollinated

A perennial herb of wasteland, roadsides, sand dunes and of the banks besides rivers and streams. The flower of the Colt's-foot closes at night and in dim weather; the leaves appear after flowering.

Yellow Iris ❀ May–July
(Iris pseudacorus) Iris Family

- Smooth stems grow up to 150cm tall
- Large bright yellow flowers with three drooping outer petals
- Long sword-shaped leaves
- Fruits are capsules containing brown seeds

Yellow Iris, also commonly known as Yellow Flag, is a tall hairless perennial of marshes, rivers, streams and ponds. The beautiful flowers of this plant form a yellow dye and the underground roots can be used to produce a black dye.

Tansy ❀ July–Sept
(Tanacetum vulgare) Daisy Family

- Grows up to 150cm tall
- Scented flowers are button-shaped, gathered in flat-topped to slightly rounded clusters
- Leaves are toothed and in alternate pairs. Each leaf is deeply cut into opposite lobes with a similar end lobe
- Fruits are nutlets without any hairs
- Insect-pollinated

A hairless perennial herb of wasteland, hedges, roadsides; also found by rivers and streams. Its leaves have been used in a variety of herbal remedies to treat worms, gout and fever.

Greater Bladderwort ✿ July–Aug
(Utricularia vulgaris) Butterwort Family

- Flowering stems grow to 30cm tall
- Yellow flowers are two-lipped with a conical spur and are gathered in stalked clusters
- Submerged leaves are divided into many thread-like strands
- Fruits are small oval capsules • Insect-pollinated

Bladderwort is a free-floating aquatic perennial of still water. This plant gains its name from the tiny bladders attached to the leaves: the bladders trap insects, and the plant digests them to obtain nutrients.

Monkey Flower ✿ July–Sept
(Mimulus guttatus) Figwort Family

- Hairy stems grow to 50cm tall
- Yellow flowers are two-lipped with tiny red spots on the three-lobed lower lip
- Leaves are oval, toothed and in opposite pairs
- Fruits are capsules

The Monkey Flower was introduced to Britain from North America in the 1800s as a garden plant, and has since escaped to become a common sight by streams, rivers and damp marshy areas.

Yellow Loosestrife ✿ July–Aug
(Lysimachia vulgaris) Primrose Family

- Stems grow to 160cm tall
- Star-shaped flowers are bright yellow with five petals and are loosely clustered on branched stalks
- Leaves are short-stalked and spear-shaped or oval and pointed, arranged in opposite pairs or in threes or fours around the stem
- Fruits are small round capsules • Insect-pollinated

Yellow Loosestrife is a downy perennial with creeping roots below the ground. It is a pretty flower that can be found in lake and river margins as well as in marshes and fens.

Lesser Spearwort ❀ May–Sept
(Ranunculus flammula) Buttercup Family

- Slender, hollow stems grow to 50cm tall
- Flowers have five shiny, golden yellow petals
- Stem leaves are spear-shaped and unstalked. Root leaves are oblong to spear-shaped and stalked
- Fruits are nutlets contained in rounded heads
- Insect-pollinated

Lesser Spearwort is a hairless perennial of ponds, lakes, ditches and other wet habitats throughout Britain. The leaves of this plant set it apart from other buttercup-like flowers. It is poisonous, with a sap that can blister the skin.

Water Forget-me-not ❀ May–Sept
(Myosotis scorpioides) Borage Family

- Grows up to 45cm tall
- Small pale blue flowers with a yellow central eye are gathered in one-sided clusters towards the top of the branched stems
- Alternate leaves are oblong to spear-shaped with a central vein
- Fruits are shiny, black nutlets held within the remaining flower parts

A creeping perennial of marshes, bogs, woodland flushes and wet meadows. The top of the flowering stems is curled under when flowers are in bud, but straightens as the flowers open.

Water Mint ❀ July–Oct
(Mentha aquatica) Mint Family

- Hairy flowering stems grow to 60cm tall
- Tiny, mauve flowers have four lobes and are gathered in domed heads and whorls around the stem
- Pointed-oval leaves are stalked or unstalked, toothed and in opposite pairs
- Fruits are nutlets held within the remaining flower parts
- Insect-pollinated

A hairy perennial herb of marshes, fens, wet woodlands and fresh water margins. The leaves smell of mint.

Skullcap
✿ June–Sept
(Scutellaria galericulata) Mint Family

- Square stems grow to 50cm tall
- Blue, tubular flowers are two-lipped with white markings on lower lip. Flowers are in pairs, growing from where the leaves meet the stem
- Toothed leaves are pointed-oval with a heart-shaped base and are in opposite pairs
- Fruits are nutlets held within the remaining flower parts • Insect-pollinated

Skullcap is a downy perennial herb with creeping underground roots. It is found in damp woodlands, fens and meadows, and by rivers and streams.

Brooklime
✿ May–Sept
(Veronica beccabunga) Figwort Family

- Grows to 60cm tall
- Small, deep blue flowers with four petals are grouped in pairs on slender stalks that emerge from where the leaves meet the stem
- Leaves are oval, fleshy, toothed and in opposite pairs
- Fruits are round, flat capsules
- Self- or insect-pollinated

Brooklime is a creeping perennial of marshes, streams, ponds and wet meadows. The young shoots of this flower are edible.

FRESH WATER HABITATS

Bulrush
✿ June–July
(Typha latifolia) Reedmace Family

- Flowering stem grows to around 250cm tall
- Flowers are minute and are held in a compact spike towards the top of the stem
- Leaves are long and pointed
- Wind-pollinated

Bulrush is a perennial that grows in the shallow waters of freshwater habitats, including ponds, rivers, streams and lakes. It is a common plant throughout most of Britain, although absent or rare in parts of Scotland.

Montbretia

🌸 July–Sept

(Tritonia x *crocosmiiflora) Iris Family*

- Slender hairless stems grow to 100cm tall
- Orange funnel-shaped flowers have six spreading petals and are gathered in long, branched one-sided clusters
- Leaves are long, narrow and pointed, and arise from the base of the plant
- Fruits are oval capsules

Montbretia is a tufted perennial with creeping stems growing in hedge banks, woodland margins and by streams. This plant is a non-native garden escapee, and is a cross between two South African species.

Marshes, Fens & Bogs

Bogbean
53

Bog Stitchwort
53

Gipsywort
53

Lesser Butterfly-
orchid 54

Hemlock Water-
dropwort 54

Common
Comfrey 54

Common
Valerian 55

Hemp-
agrimony 55

Wild Angelica
55

Cuckooflower
56

Common
Hemp-nettle 56

Ragged-robin
56

Great
Willow-herb 57

Marsh
Woundwort 57

Purple
Loosestrife 57

Marsh
Cinquefoil 58

MARSHES, FENS & BOGS

| 51 |

Marsh Thistle
58

**Devil's-bit
Scabious** 58

Skullcap
59

Brooklime
59

**Heath
Dog-violet** 59

**Water Forget-
me-not** 60

Marsh Violet
60

Bog Asphodel
60

**Common
Cow-wheat** 61

Marsh-marigold
61

**Lesser
Spearwort** 61

**Celery-leaved
Buttercup** 62

Yellow Iris
62

**Perennial
Sow-thistle** 62

Common Nettle
63

**Marsh
Pennywort** 63

Bogbean

❀ May–July

(Menyanthes trifoliata) Bogbean Family

- Leafless stems grow to 40cm tall
- White star-shaped flowers have five petals that are flushed pink on the underside and covered in long white hairs
- Hairless leaves are on long stalks and divided into three oval leaflets
- Fruits are oval capsules • Insect-pollinated

Bogbean is a creeping perennial of bogs, ponds, lakes and marshes. The leaves of this plant were once used in the process of beer making, and the roots pounded to make a kind of flour.

Bog Stitchwort

❀ May–June

(Stellaria uliginosa) Campion Family

- Square stems grow to 60cm tall
- Small white flowers have five deeply divided petals that are shorter than sepals, and are solitary on slender stems or in loose clusters
- Small greyish-green leaves are one-veined, stalkless and in opposite pairs
- Insect-pollinated

Bog Stitchwort is a perennial of marshes, woodland flushes and grassy streamsides, preferring acid soils.

Gipsywort

❀ June–Sept

(Lycopus europaeus) Mint Family

- Square stems grow to 100cm tall
- Small, white bell-shaped flowers have purple dots on the lower of the four lobes. Flowers are arranged in whorls around the stem at the base of each pair of leaves
- Spear-shaped leaves are deeply toothed and in opposite pairs along the stem
- Fruits are four individual nutlets held within the remaining flower parts • Insect-pollinated

Gipsywort is a hairy perennial herb that is found beside streams, rivers, ponds, ditches and some wet woodlands, favouring fertile and peaty soils.

MARSHES, FENS & BOGS

Lesser Butterfly-orchid   ✿ May–July
(Platanthera bifolia) Orchid Family

- Single stems grow to 40cm tall
- Scented white flowers with a slight green tinge have long spurs and are grouped together in a loose spike
- Two broad oval leaves at base of plant. Stem leaves are small and scale-like
- Fruits are capsules • Pollinated by moths

A hairless perennial of heath land, bogs, fens and woodlands. It is very like the Greater Butterfly-orchid, but has smaller flowers which have less of a green tinge.

Hemlock Water-dropwort   ✿ June–Sept
(Oenanthe crocata) Carrot Family

- Hairless, hollow stems up to 150cm tall
- Tiny white flowers clustered in dome-shaped heads up to 15cm across
- Leaf triangular overall and divided into 3–4 pairs of deeply wedged leaflets

Hemlock Water-dropwort is a hairless perennial that can be found throughout Britain (although rare to the east and in Scotland), by ditches, lakes, rivers and streams. The whole of this plant is very poisonous and has been used in the past as a rat poison.

Common Comfrey   ✿ May–June
(Symphytum officinale) Borage Family

- Grows up to 120cm tall
- White or pink flowers are tubular to narrowly bell-shaped and are gathered in loose drooping clusters at the end of branched stems
- Leaves at the base of the plant are stalked and broadly spear-shaped
- Stem leaves are smaller, narrower and can be in wing-like pairs
- Fruits are shiny black nutlets • Insect-pollinated

A perennial flower growing beside, rivers, streams, marshes and ditches. Very nutrient-rich; seen in many allotments, where it is used as compost.

Common Valerian

🌸 June–Aug

(Valeriana officinalis) Valerian Family

- Grooved stems grow to 120cm tall
- Small, scented, pinkish-white flowers with five petals are grouped together at the top of branched stems
- Opposite leaves are divided into pairs of toothed spear-shaped leaflets with a similar end leaflet. Lower stem leaves are stalked.
- Fruits are one-seeded with white hairs at the top
- Insect-pollinated

Common Valerian is a perennial of riversides, fens, marshes and damp woodlands. This plant has been used in the past as a sedative.

Hemp-agrimony

🌸 July–Sept

(Eupatorium cannabinum) Daisy Family

- Flushed red stems grow to 120cm tall
- Tiny pink flowers are tightly grouped together on branched stems to form slightly domed heads
- Leaves are in opposite pairs and divided into three to five toothed, spear-shaped leaflets
- Fruits are black nutlets topped with white hairs
- Insect-pollinated

A downy perennial that grows throughout Britain on marshes, fens, wet woodlands and hedgerows; quite rare in some northern parts of Scotland.

Wild Angelica

🌸 June–Sept

(Angelica sylvestris) Carrot Family

- Grooved stems are flushed purple and grow to 200cm tall
- Minute pink or white flowers are gathered in stalked clusters forming dome-shaped heads up to 15cm across
- Leaves are divided into 2–3 pairs of pointed, oval and toothed leaflets, with an end leaflet. There are broad sheaths at the base of the stems

An erect hairless perennial found by streams, rivers, lakes, ditches, wet meadows, marshes and fens preferring more calcareous soils. Has been used to produce a yellow dye as well as a flavouring.

MARSHES, FENS & BOGS

Cuckooflower ❀ April–June
(Cardamine pratensis) Cabbage Family

- Grows to 50cm tall
- Pink-white flowers have four petals and yellow anthers and are gathered in loose clusters towards the top of the stem
- Slightly hairy leaves are divided into opposite pairs of rounded leaflets with a larger, kidney-shaped end leaflet
- Fruits are straight, narrow pods
- Insect-pollinated

A perennial herb of damp woodlands, streamsides and damp grassy places such as meadows and some gardens. Also known as Lady's Smock.

Common Hemp-nettle ❀ July–Sept
(Galeopsis tetrahit) Mint Family

- Square, hairy stems grow to 100cm tall
- Pink flowers are two-lipped with purplish markings on the lobed lower lip. Flowers arranged in whorls around leafy stems
- Leaves are in opposite pairs, oval and pointed
- Fruits are nutlets held within the remaining flower parts • Self-pollinated

Common Hemp-nettle is a branched, erect annual of arable and cultivated land, hedgerows, woodlands and fens.

Ragged-robin ❀ May–Aug
(Lychnis flos-cuculi) Campion Family

- Grows up to 100cm tall
- Deep pink flowers with five petals that are deeply divided into four narrow lobes
- All leaves are in opposite pairs. Stem leaves are narrow and pointed whilst lower leaves are oblong and larger
- Fruits are capsules • Insect-pollinated

This hairless perennial grows in wet and damp places in meadows, fens, marshes and woodlands. The clove-like scent draws in bumblebees and butterflies by day and moths by night.

MARSHES, FENS & BOGS

Great Willow-herb   ❀ July–Aug
(Epilobium hirsutum) Willowherb Family

- Downy perennial growing to 150cm tall
- Purplish-pink flowers are held in loose branched clusters
- Shallowly toothed leaves are in opposite pairs and slightly clasping the stems
- Fruits are long slender capsules
- Self- or insect-pollinated

Grows on marshes, fens and by the sides of streams, rivers, ponds and ditches. The seeds that are contained within the capsules have white hairs attached to them that aid their dispersal by the wind.

Marsh Woundwort   ❀ July–Sept
(Stachys palustris) Mint Family

- Square, hollow stems grow to 100cm tall
- Pinkish-purple flowers are two-lipped with white markings on lower lip and are in whorls around the stem above each pair of leaves
- Opposite pairs of toothed leaves are stalked on lower stem and stalkless above
- Fruits are nutlets that are held within the remaining flower parts • Pollinated by bees

A hairy perennial with creeping underground roots. It is a plant of marshes and freshwater margins throughout most of Britain, although quite scarce in some highland parts of Scotland.

Purple-loosestrife   ❀ June–Aug
(Lythrum salicaria)
Purple-loosestrife Family

- Angled stems grow to 150cm tall
- Red-purple flowers (up to 1.5cm across) with six petals, grouped together in long spikes up to 30cm long
- Leaves are pointed-oval in opposite pairs or in threes. Leaves become smaller up the stem
- Fruits are oval capsules • Insect-pollinated

Purple-loosestrife is a downy perennial found in marshes and by the sides of rivers and streams throughout Britain, apart from the far north of Scotland.

MARSHES, FENS & BOGS

Marsh Cinquefoil
🌼 May–June
(Potentilla palustris) Rose Family

- Grows to 50cm tall
- Reddish-purple flowers with many stamens have five petals and five large pointed sepals (twice the size of the petals)
- Stalked leaves divided into 5–7 toothed leaflets that are paler underneath
- Purple one-seeded fruits • Insect-pollinated

Marsh Cinquefoil is a distinctive perennial of marshes, fens, bogs and wet meadows.

Marsh Thistle
🌼 July–Sept
(Cirsium palustre) Daisy Family

- Hairy, spiny, few branched stems grow to 150cm tall
- Many purple florets emerge from egg-shaped heads that are covered in green-purplish bracts and are gathered in compact leafy clusters at the end of the stem
- Leaves are deeply lobed with spiny edges and hairy above • Insect-pollinated

Marsh Thistle is a biennial of marshes, damp grassland and woodlands. This plant can also have white flowers.

Devil's-bit Scabious
🌼 June–Oct
(Succisa pratensis) Scabious Family

- Grows up to 100cm tall
- Tiny, four-lobed, purplish-blue flowers with long protruding stamens are tightly packed together in domed heads
- Leaves are pointed-oval with a central vein. Stem leaves are in opposite pairs whilst the leaves at the base of the plant are in a rosette
- Fruits are one-seeded • Insect-pollinated

Devil's-bit Scabious is a slightly hairy perennial of marshes, fens, heaths, wet meadows and streamsides. This plant was used in the past as a cure for scabies.

Skullcap
(Scutellaria galericulata) Mint Family

🌸 June–Sept

- Square stems grow to 50cm tall
- Blue, tubular flowers are two-lipped with white markings on lower lip. Flowers are in pairs, growing from where the leaves meet the stem
- Toothed leaves are pointed-oval with a heart-shaped base and are in opposite pairs
- Fruits are nutlets held within the remaining flower parts • Insect-pollinated

Skullcap is a downy perennial herb with creeping underground roots. It is found in damp woodlands, fens and meadows, and by rivers and streams.

Brooklime
(Veronica beccabunga) Figwort Family

🌸 May–Sept

- Grows to 60cm tall
- Small, deep blue flowers with four petals are grouped in pairs on slender stalks that emerge from where the leaves meet the stem
- Leaves are oval, fleshy, toothed and in opposite pairs
- Fruits are round, flat capsules
- Self- or insect-pollinated

Brooklime is a creeping perennial of marshes, streams, ponds and wet meadows. The young shoots of this flower are edible.

Heath Dog-violet
(Viola canina) Violet Family

🌸 April–July

- Grows to 15cm tall
- Nodding blue flowers with five petals and a yellow spur are solitary on stems
- Toothed leaves are pointed-oval or heart-shaped and on long stalks
- Insect-pollinated • Fruits are capsules

Heath Dog-violet is a perennial of dry acid grassland, fens and heaths. The seeds of this flower are dispersed as the capsules shrink.

MARSHES, FENS & BOGS

Water Forget-me-not ❀ May–Sept
(Myosotis scorpioides) Borage Family

- Grows up to 45cm tall
- Small pale blue flowers with a yellow central eye are gathered in one-sided clusters towards the top of the branched stems
- Alternate leaves are oblong to spear-shaped with a central vein
- Fruits are shiny, black nutlets held within the remaining flower parts

A creeping perennial of marshes, bogs, woodland flushes and wet meadows. The top of the flowering stems is curled under when flowers are in bud, but straightens as the flowers open.

Marsh Violet ❀ April–July
(Viola palustris) Violet Family

- Grows to 15cm tall
- Nodding lilac flowers with five purple-veined petals are solitary on long slender stalks emerging from creeping underground roots
- Leaves are kidney-shaped, long stalked and shallowly toothed
- Fruits are capsules • Insect-pollinated

Marsh Violet is a pretty perennial flower of marshes, bogs and woodland flushes.

Bog Asphodel ❀ July–Aug
(Narthecium ossifragum) Lily Family

- Grooved stem grow to 40cm tall
- Yellow, star-shaped flowers have six petals and are gathered in a flowering spike
- Leaves at the base of the plant are long and narrow. Stem leaves are much smaller and almost lie flat against the stem
- Fruits are oval capsules
- Self- or insect-pollinated

A hairless perennial of bogs and wet heaths across Britain although becoming quite rare in places due to loss of habitat.

Common Cow-wheat
✿ May–Sept
(Melampyrum pratense) Figwort Family

- Grows to 60cm tall
- Pairs of two-lipped pale yellow flowers arranged in one-sided leafy spikes
- Leaves are in opposite pairs, short-stalked, pointed-oval or spear-shaped
- Fruits are small capsules

Common Cow-wheat is an annual of bogs, woodland clearings and heath land. This plant is partially parasitic, obtaining nutrients from the roots of trees, heather and shrubs.

Marsh-marigold
✿ March–June
(Caltha palustris) Buttercup Family

- Hollow, grooved stems grow to 40cm tall
- Yellow flowers with five shiny petals (actually sepals) and many stamens
- Dark green leaves are toothed and heart-shaped. Lower leaves are stalked, with upper leaves clasping the stem
- Seeds are contained in pods
- Insect-pollinated

Also known as Kingcup, this perennial is the large buttercup-like flower of marshes, fens, woodland flushes, streamsides and wet meadows.

Lesser Spearwort
✿ May–Sept
(Ranunculus flammula) Buttercup Family

- Slender, hollow stems grow to 50cm tall
- Flowers have five shiny, golden yellow petals
- Stem leaves are spear-shaped and unstalked. Root leaves are oblong to spear-shaped and stalked
- Fruits are nutlets contained in rounded heads
- Insect-pollinated

Lesser Spearwort is a hairless perennial of ponds, lakes, ditches and other wet habitats throughout Britain. The leaves of this plant set it apart from other buttercup-like flowers. It is poisonous, with a sap that can blister the skin.

MARSHES, FENS & BOGS

Celery-leaved Buttercup ❀ May–Sept
(Ranunculus sceleratus) Buttercup Family

- Hollow branched stems grow to 60cm tall
- Small flowers have five shiny, pale yellow petals
- Leaves are pale green and shiny. Leaves at the bottom of the plant are on long stalks and divided into three broad, deeply toothed lobes. Stem leaves are narrower and less toothed
- Fruits are nutlets contained in rounded heads
- Insect-pollinated

A hairless annual found on the muddy verges of lakes, rivers and ponds as well as wet meadows. The whole of this plant is poisonous, with a sap that can blister the skin.

Yellow Iris ❀ May–July
(Iris pseudacorus) Iris Family

- Smooth stems grow up to 150cm tall
- Large bright yellow flowers with three drooping outer petals
- Long sword-shaped leaves
- Fruits are capsules containing brown seeds

A tall hairless perennial of marshes, rivers, streams and ponds, also commonly known as Yellow Flag. The beautiful flowers of this plant form a yellow dye and the underground roots can be used to produce a black dye.

Perennial Sow-thistle ❀ July–Oct
(Sonchus arvensis) Daisy Family

- Grows to 150cm tall
- Loose clusters of single yellow flowers are on sticky yellow hairy stalks
- Leaves are deeply lobed and edged with spines. Upper leaves clasp the stem
- Fruits are brown seeds with a top of white hairs
- Insect-pollinated

A stout hairy perennial with hollow stems and dandelion-like flowers. This plant can be found in fens, waste ground, cultivated and arable land, and by streams and rivers.

Common Nettle
❀ June–Aug
(Urtica dioica) Nettle Family

- Hairy stems grow to 150cm tall
- Tiny green flowers without petals are grouped together in drooping clusters emerging from the base of the leaf stalks
- Stalked leaves are toothed, pointed with a heart-shaped base
- Wind-pollinated

A hairy perennial that grows well in many habitats such as wasteland, woodlands, hedge banks, roadsides and fens, and by rivers and streams. Both the stem and leaves are covered in stinging hairs that irritate the skin on contact.

Marsh Pennywort
❀ June–Aug
(Hydrocotyle vulgaris) Carrot Family

- Leaf stalks grow up to 20cm tall
- Minute pinkish-green flowers are stalkless and in whorls around the stem
- Round leaves are on long stalks and slightly toothed
- Fruits are tiny round, flattish capsules
- Self-pollinated

Marsh Pennywort is a creeping perennial of bogs and marshes, also found by streams and other wet areas.

Heaths & Moors

Goldenrod
69

Leafy
Hawkweed 69

Mouse-ear
Hawkweed 69

Common Bird's-
foot-trefoil 70

Tormentil
70

Gorse
70

Broom
71

Slender St
John's-wort 71

Common
Cow-wheat 71

Wood Sage
72

Round-leaved
Sundew 72

Wind Eyebright
72

Bilberry
73

Lousewort
73

Cross-leaved
Heath 73

Heath Spotted-
orchid 74

Wild Thyme
74

Heather
74

Bell Heather
75

**Marsh
Cinquefoil** 75

Sheep's Sorrel
75

**Heath
Speedwell** 76

Harebell
76

Heath Milkwort
76

HEATHS & MOORS

Goldenrod
❀ July–Sept
(Solidago virgaurea) Daisy Family

- Grows to 100cm tall
- Yellow flowers have both disc and ray florets and are gathered in long leafy spikes
- Leaves at the base of the plant are dark green, stalked and slightly toothed. Stem leaves are narrower, spear-shaped and un-stalked
- Fruits are heads of brown nutlets with a top of hairs • Insect- or self-pollinated

A slightly hairy perennial herb with few-branching stems that grows on dry grassland, heaths, hedgebanks and woodlands. The flowers and leaves can be used to produce a yellow dye.

Leafy Hawkweed
❀ June–Oct
(Hieracium umbellatum) Daisy Family

- Branched stems grow to 80cm tall
- Yellow flowers consisting of rays of florets and scale-like bracts that are curved back at the tip. Flowers are in flat-topped clusters
- Stalkless leaves are narrow to spear-shaped, slightly toothed or un-toothed and are mostly alternate
- Fruits are heads of nutlets with a top of white hairs

A hairy perennial of dry grasslands, heaths, roadsides and open woodlands throughout Britain.

Mouse-ear Hawkweed
❀ May–Sept
(Pilosella officinarum) Daisy Family

- Hairy leafless flowering stems grow to 25cm
- Yellow flowers consisting of rays of florets are solitary with red streaks on the underside
- Hairy leaves are spoon-shaped, pale underneath and in a rosette at the base of the plant
- Fruits are heads of dark nutlets with a top of white hairs

Mouse-ear Hawkweed is a perennial with creeping leafy stems and is commonly found on wasteland, heaths, grassland, lawns, walls and grassy banks.

HEATHS & MOORS

Common Bird's-foot-trefoil
❀ June–Sept
(Lotus corniculatus) Pea Family

- Grows up to 40cm tall
- Golden yellow flowers are two-lipped and sometimes flushed red or orange. Up to eight flowers are gathered at the top of a long stalk
- Leaves are divided into five pointed-oval leaflets
- Fruits are long pods that are arranged like a 'bird's foot' • Insect-pollinated

Bird's-foot Trefoil is a perennial of short grasslands, roadsides, cliffs and coastal areas of Britain. Has many local names such as 'bacon and eggs' and 'ham and eggs'.

Tormentil
❀ June–Sept
(Potentilla erecta) Rose Family

- Slender stems grow to around 20cm tall
- Yellow flowers have four petals and are on long stalks that emerge from where upper leaves meet the stem
- Leaves are divided into five toothed leaflets
- Hairless one-seeded fruits are contained in rounded heads

Tormentil is a creeping or erect perennial that at a glance can look like a four petalled buttercup. It is a plant of grasslands, open woodlands, heaths and moors, avoiding chalky or lime-rich soils.

Gorse
❀ mainly April–Oct
(Ulex europaeus) Pea Family

- Stems up to 300cm tall
- Scented yellow flowers are in clusters towards the end of spiny branches
- Young shrubs have leaves that are small and divided into three leaflets. Older shrubs develop sharp branched spines
- Fruits are hairy, black, flattish pods
- Insect-pollinated

Gorse is an evergreen spiny shrub of sea cliffs, heathland, open woodlands and wasteland. The seeds of this plant can lay dormant in the ground for many years before germinating.

Broom
(Cytisus scoparius) Pea Family
❀ May–June

- Angled stems grow up to 300cm tall
- Scented golden yellow flowers are two-lipped and gathered along the branched leafy stems
- Small leaves (smaller than flowers) are short stalked and divided into three leaflets
- Fruits are flattish, black, hairy pods
- Insect-pollinated

Broom is a shrub without spines (like Gorse) of wasteland, roadsides, railway banks, scrubland and heaths throughout Britain. The pods of this flower burst when ripe, helping dispersal.

Slender St John's-wort
(Hypericum pulchrum)
St John's-wort Family
❀ June–Aug

- Slender stems, often flushed red, grow to around 80cm tall
- Yellow flowers have five petals and five sepals with black dots, and are gathered in loose branched clusters
- Stalkless oval leaves are in opposite pairs and covered in translucent dots
- Fruits are three-celled capsules

A hairless perennial of grasslands, heaths and open woodlands and scrubland.

Common Cow-wheat
(Melampyrum pratense) Figwort Family
❀ May–Sept

- Grows to 60cm tall
- Pairs of two-lipped pale yellow flowers arranged in one-sided leafy spikes
- Leaves are in opposite pairs, short-stalked, pointed-oval or spear-shaped
- Fruits are small capsules

Common Cow-wheat is an annual of bogs, woodland clearings and heath land. This plant is partially parasitic, obtaining nutrients from the roots of trees, heather and shrubs.

HEATHS & MOORS

Wood Sage   🌼 June–Sept
(Teucrium scorodonia) Mint Family

- Grows to 60cm tall
- Yellowish-green flowers with only a lower lobed lip are in opposite pairs and grouped in branched spikes
- Toothed leaves have a wrinkled surface, are heart-shaped at the base and in opposite pairs up the stem
- Fruits are nutlets • Insect-pollinated

A downy perennial herb with square stems that are often flushed red. It is a flower of open woodlands, sand dunes, rough grasslands and heaths.

Round-leaved Sundew   🌼 June–Aug
(Drosera rotundifolia) Sundew Family

- Leafless stems grow to 15cm tall
- Tiny white flowers have six petals and are gathered in long clusters towards the end of the stem
- Small long-stalked leaves are in a basal rosette and are covered in sticky, red, glandular hairs
- Fruits are tiny capsules • Self-pollinated

A perennial common on wet peaty areas of heaths and bogs. It is a distinctive plant which obtains extra nutrients by digesting insects that become trapped in the sticky hairs of its leaves.

Wind Eyebright   🌼 July–Sept
(Euphrasia nemorosa) Figwort Family

- Branched stems grow up to 20cm tall
- Tiny white two-lipped flowers have purple streaks and a yellow patch on a lower three-lobed lip
- Dark green leaves often flushed purple are toothed, stalkless and in opposite pairs
- Fruits are small capsules • Insect-pollinated

An annual herb of short grasslands, heaths and open woodland, which has been used in a variety of herbal remedies for eye complaints. Many species of Eyebright grow in Britain, and it is quite difficult to distinguish between them.

Bilberry ✿ April–July
(Vaccinium myrtillus) Heath Family

- Angled stems grow to 60cm tall
- Green-pinkish flowers are round and inflated; solitary or in pairs on short stalks that emerge from where the leaf meets the stem
- Alternate leaves are oval, pointed and toothed
- Fruits are dark blue to black berries
- Insect-pollinated

A deciduous shrub of heath, moors and some open woodlands. The fruits are picked in July and can be eaten raw or used to make jam.

Lousewort ✿ April–July
(Pedicularis sylvatica) Figwort Family

- Hairless un-branched stems grow to 25cm tall
- Flowers are pink, two-lipped, open, with few flowers held in loose leafy clusters
- Alternating leaves are cut into many opposite and toothed lobes with a similar end lobe
- Fruits are capsules that are held in the remaining flower parts • Insect-pollinated

A perennial with many stems that grow along the ground before rising upwards; a plant of marshes, bogs, damp grassland, damp heaths and woodland flushes. It is partially parasitic, taking its food and water from the roots of other plants.

Cross-leaved Heath ✿ June–Sept
(Erica tetralix) Heath Family

- Grows to 30cm tall
- Pink, egg-shaped flowers are in nodding clusters at the end of leafy stems
- Many tiny greyish-green leaves are covered in bristles and are in whorls of four around the stem
- Fruits are capsules

Cross-leaved Heath is an evergreen shrub with few branching stems that can be found in acid soil on heaths, bogs and moors.

HEATHS & MOORS

Heath Spotted-orchid ❀ May–Aug
(Dactylorhiza maculata) Orchid Family

- Smooth solitary stems grow to 50cm tall
- Pink flowers have dark pink-purple markings and a broad shallowly lobed lower lip. Flowers are gathered in cone-shaped spikes
- Leaves are long, narrow, pointed and covered in purple rounded spots. Leaves further up the stem are smaller and lie close to the stem
- Fruits are twisted capsules • Insect-pollinated

A stout perennial of heaths, moors, bogs and acid grassland. The Common Spotted Orchid is a similar plant but has blunt, broader leaves and flowers that have a more deeply lobed lower lip.

Wild Thyme ❀ May–Aug
(Thymus polytrichus) Mint Family

- Square hairy stems grow to 10cm tall
- Tiny pink to purplish-pink flowers are two-lipped and grouped together in round spikes
- Leaves are spear-shaped and in opposite pairs up the stem
- Fruits are four nutlets held within the remaining flower parts • Insect-pollinated

An aromatic perennial herb found in short chalk grassland, coastal heaths, rocks, and sand dunes of Britain. It is a mat-forming plant with a distinctive smell and hairs only on two opposite sides of the square stem.

Heather ❀ July–Sept
(Calluna vulgaris) Heath Family

- Many branching stems grow to around 60cm
- Tiny pinkish-purple, bell-shaped flowers are clustered in branched leafy spikes
- Tiny, overlapping leaves are in four rows lying close to the stem
- Fruits are tiny capsules
- Wind- or insect-pollinated

Heather, also known as Ling, is an evergreen shrub that can be found in large numbers on heaths, moors, open woodlands and some bogs.

Bell Heather
✿ July–Sept
(Erica cinerea) Heath Family

- Grows to 60cm tall
- Tiny, reddish-purple flowers are egg-shaped and held in clusters towards the top of the leafy stems
- Tiny, narrow, dark green leaves are in many whorls of threes around the branched stems
- Fruits are tiny capsules
- Insect- or self-pollinated

An evergreen shrub with woody branching stems and can be found on dry heaths and moors throughout Britain. The flowers of this plant can also be found in white.

Marsh Cinquefoil
✿ May–June
(Potentilla palustris) Rose Family

- Grows to 50cm tall
- Reddish-purple flowers with many stamens have five petals and five large pointed sepals (twice the size of the petals)
- Stalked leaves divided into 5–7 toothed leaflets that are paler underneath
- Purple one-seeded fruits • Insect-pollinated

Marsh Cinquefoil is a distinctive perennial of marshes, fens, bogs and wet meadows.

Sheep's Sorrel
✿ May–Sept
(Rumex acetosella) Dock Family

- Branched flowering stems grow to 70cm tall
- Flowers are tiny, red and gathered in slender spikes
- Fleshy leaves are oval, pointed with opposite narrow lobes at the base. Stem leaves are on stalks with stem leaves clasping the stem
- Fruits are tiny nutlets
- Wind-pollinated

Sheep's Sorrel is a hairless perennial of short dry grassland, roadside verges, shingle beaches and heaths. The whole of this plant has been used to treat a variety of kidney complaints.

HEATHS & MOORS

Heath Speedwell
❀ May–Aug
(Veronica officinalis) Figwort Family

- Hairy stems grow to 25cm tall
- Light blue to lilac flowers have four petals with darker streaks and are gathered in dense, short stalked spikes
- Toothed leaves are oval, hairy and in opposite pairs up the stem
- Fruits are small hairy capsules
- Insect-pollinated

Heath Speedwell is a perennial with creeping underground stems of dry grasslands, open woodlands and heaths.

Harebell
❀ July–Oct
(Campanula rotundifolia)
Bellflower Family

- Slender flowering stems grow to 40cm tall
- Blue, nodding bell-shaped flowers
- Leaves at base of flower are toothed, long stalked and rounded with a heart-shaped base; stem leaves are narrow, short stalked or stalkless and less toothed.
- Fruits are rounded capsules
- Self- or insect-pollinated

A delicate-looking hairless perennial of fixed sand dunes, dry grasslands, hedgerows and heaths throughout Britain.

Heath Milkwort
❀ May–Sept
(Polygala serpyllifolia) Milkwort Family

- Branched stems grow to around 30cm tall
- Small deep blue flowers have five petal-like sepals with three small real petals and are gathered in short-stalked clusters along the stem
- Small pointed leaves are spear-shaped are in opposite pairs on the lower stem; alternate pairs above
- Fruits are two-celled capsules

Heath Milkwort is a hairless perennial of heaths, moors and acid grassland. The flowers of this plant can also be found in purple, pink or white.

HEATHS & MOORS

Grassland & Meadows

Oxeye Daisy
85

Daisy
85

Lesser Stitchwort 85

Common Mouse-ear 86

Pignut
86

Bladder Campion 86

Meadowsweet
87

Wild Strawberry 87

White Clover
87

Wild Carrot
88

Hogweed
88

Wind Eyebright
88

Star-of-Bethlehem 89

Fairy Flax
89

Yarrow
89

Wild Angelica
90

Dropwort
90

Cuckooflower
90

Common Centaury 91

Common Restharrow 91

Lousewort
91

Red Bartsia
92

Comm. Spotted-orchid 92

Fragrant Orchid
92

Bog Pimpernel
93

Dove's-foot Crane's-bill 93

Cut-leaved Crane's-bill 93

Ragged-robin
94

Marjoram
94

Wild Thyme
94

Common Vetch
95

Autumn Gentian 95

Betony
95

Common
Knapweed 96

Marsh Thistle
96

Lucerne
96

Devil's-bit
Scabious 97

Tufted Vetch
97

Bugle
97

Common
Milkwort 98

Skullcap
98

Selfheal
98

Brooklime
99

Harebell
99

Chicory
99

Germander
Speedwell 100

Slender
Speedwell 100

Meadow
Crane's-bill 100

Field Scabious 101

Heath Speedwell 101

Common Cornsalad 101

Creeping Thistle 102

Marsh-marigold 102

Meadow Buttercup 102

Creeping Buttercup 103

Bulbous Buttercup 103

Agrimony 103

Silverweed 104

Tormentil 104

Creeping Cinquefoil 104

Common Toadflax 105

Yellow Rattle 105

Common Ragwort 105

Dandelion 106

Cat's-ear
106

Lesser Hawkbit
106

Autumn Hawkbit 107

Goat's-beard
107

Leafy Hawkweed 107

Mouse-ear Hawkweed 108

Meadow Vetchling 108

Black Medick
108

Hop Trefoil
109

Lesser Trefoil
109

Common Bird's-foot-trefoil 109

Kidney Vetch
110

Slender St John's-wort 110

Perforate St John's-wort 110

Common Rock-rose 111

Wild Parsnip
111

Cowslip
111

Creeping Jenny
112

Lady's Bedstraw
112

Marsh
Cudweed 112

Wood Sage
113

Common
Twayblade 113

Salad Burnet
113

Scarlet
Pimpernel 114

Common Sorrel
114

Sheep's Sorrel
114

Oxeye Daisy ❀ May–Sept
(Leucanthemum vulgare) Daisy Family

- Slightly grooved stems grow to 90cm tall
- Solitary white flowers with a yellow centre and a ray of white florets
- Toothed leaves are stalked and spoon-shaped at the base. Stem leaves are smaller, narrower and stalkless
- Fruits are heads of hairless nutlets
- Insect-pollinated

A large daisy-like perennial herb of grasslands, meadows, roadsides and open woodlands. The whole of this plant can be used to make herbal tonics and infusions.

Daisy ❀ March–Dec
(Bellis perennis) Daisy Family

- Hairy, leafless, flowering stems grow to 15cm tall
- Solitary flowers with a yellow central disc of florets and an outer ray of white florets that are often tinged red underneath
- Leaves are short-stalked, spoon-shaped and are gathered in a low-lying rosette at the base of the plant
- Fruits are heads of downy nutlets

Daisy is a hairy perennial herb of garden lawns and other places with short grass throughout Britain. The long-stemmed flowers are picked by children to make daisy chains.

Lesser Stitchwort ❀ May–Aug
(Stellaria graminea) Campion Family

- Grows to 60cm tall
- White flowers with five deeply divided petals, few flowers are gathered in loose stalked clusters
- Small, pointed leaves are narrow, spear-shaped, and are in opposite pairs
- Fruits are round capsules • Insect-pollinated

A hairless perennial herb with slender square stems. It is a wild flower of grassland, hedge-banks, heaths and woodland clearings, preferring acid ground. It is a similar plant to Greater Stitchwort but has smaller flowers, more deeply divided petals and smaller leaves.

Common Mouse-ear
❀ April–Oct
(Cerastium fontanum) Campion Family

- Slender hairy stems grow to 30cm tall
- Small white flowers have five deeply notched petals and are gathered in loose branched clusters
- Narrow-oval leaves with a central vein are hairy and in opposite pairs
- Fruits are curved capsules
- Self- or insect-pollinated

Common Mouse-ear is a perennial of wasteland, roadsides, grassland, sand dunes and meadows.

Pignut
❀ May–June
(Conopodium majus) Carrot Family

- Grows up to 80cm tall
- Tiny flowers have five petals, gathered in domed stalked clusters
- Leaves are divided into feather-like segments towards the base of the plant, and soon wither

Pignut, also known as Earth Nut, is a perennial herb of woodlands, hedge banks and old grassland. The English names of this pretty flower derive from the rounded, underground tuber that was once eaten by foraging pigs.

Bladder Campion
❀ May–Sept
(Silene vulgaris) Campion Family

- Branched stems grow to 90cm tall
- White scented flowers with five deeply divided petals. Each flower has a ribbed, greenish-cream oval sac
- Leaves are oval, pointed, in opposite pairs; those on lower stems are stalked
- Fruits are capsules • Insect-pollinated

A perennial herb of dry grassy places including cultivated and arable land, wasteland, roadsides and hedgerows, preferring sandy calcareous soils. The inflated sac that gives the flower its name is formed from the fused sepals known as the calyx.

Meadowsweet ❀ June–Sept
(Filipendula ulmaria) Rose Family

- Stems are often flushed red and grow to 150cm
- Tiny scented flowers are white with five petals and are densely gathered in branched clusters
- Scented leaves are divided into pairs of toothed leaflets with a smaller pair of toothed leaflets between and a toothed end leaflet
- Fruits are small pods twisted together in groups of up to ten

Meadowsweet is a hairy perennial herb of damp grasslands, meadows and fens, and is also found by rivers and streams. The densely grouped flowers look almost fluffy from afar.

Wild Strawberry ❀ April–July
(Fragaria vesca) Rose Family

- Grows up to 30cm tall
- White flowers have five petals and a yellow centre
- Shiny leaves are on long stalks and divided into three toothed leaflets
- Distinctive fruits are fleshy and red

Wild Strawberry is a creeping perennial herb of dry grasslands, scrub, wasteland and open woodlands. The fruits are instantly recognisable, but are smaller than the variety of strawberry normally found in shops.

White Clover ❀ June–Sept
(Trifolium repens) Pea Family

- Leafless flowering stems grow to 20cm tall
- Tiny white scented florets are grouped together to form characteristic rounded heads
- Leaves are long-stalked and divided into three rounded-oval leaflets. Each leaflet has a white arrow-shaped marking
- Fruits are round heads of brown pods
- Insect-pollinated

Also known as Dutch Clover, this is a hairless perennial with long, creeping, rooting stems. It grows well on grasslands, garden lawns and wasteland. Has been cultivated as a fodder crop.

Wild Carrot ✤ June–Aug
(Daucus carota) Carrot Family

- Hairy grooved stems grow to 100cm tall
- Tiny white flowers are tightly grouped together to form domed umbels; the central flower of the domed head is usually red. At the base of the flower head is a ruff of deeply divided, narrow leaf-like bracts
- Leaves are stalked and divided into deeply cut fern-like leaflets
- Tiny, oval and hairy one-seeded fruits

A hairy biennial growing on grasslands, road-sides, hedgerows and coastal areas. The leaves smell of carrot when crushed.

Hogweed ✤ June–Sept
(Heracleum sphondylium) Carrot Family

- Grooved stems, sometimes flushed red, grow to 200cm tall
- Tiny white or pinkish flowers are tightly grouped together in umbels up to 25cm across
- Leaves are divided into large deeply lobed and toothed leaflets
- Oval, flat and smooth one-seeded fruits

Hogweed is a large biennial of woodlands, hedgerows, roadsides, streamsides and rough grasslands of Britain. The sap is hazardous: it can burn and blister the skin in sunlight.

Wind Eyebright ✤ July–Sept
(Euphrasia nemorosa) Figwort Family

- Branched stems grow up to 20cm tall
- Tiny white two-lipped flowers have purple streaks and a yellow patch on a lower three-lobed lip
- Dark green leaves often flushed purple are toothed, stalkless and in opposite pairs
- Fruits are small capsules • Insect-pollinated

An annual herb of short grasslands, heaths and open woodland, which has been used in a variety of herbal remedies for eye complaints. Many species of Eyebright grow in Britain, and it is quite difficult to distinguish between them.

Star-of-Bethlehem
🌸 April–June
(Ornithogalum angustifolum) Lily Family

- Stems grow to 30cm tall
- White cup-shaped to star-like flowers with six petals and a green stripe on the underside
- Long narrow leaves up to 30cm have a white stripe down the centre
- Fruits are capsules

Common Star-of-Bethlehem is a hairless perennial with edible bulbs found in dry grassland, wasteland and roadside verges. The flowers of this pretty plant open at around mid-morning.

Fairy Flax
🌸 June–Sept
(Linum catharticum) Flax Family

- Slender forked flowering stems up to 15cm tall
- White flowers with five petals are in loose nodding clusters
- Leaves are blunt, oval-oblong, stalkless and in opposite pairs up the delicate stems
- Fruits are round capsules
- Insect-pollinated

A delicate annual of cliff-tops, sand dunes, and grasslands, preferring limestone and chalk soils. Another common name is Purging Flax, probably due to its past use as a purgative.

Yarrow
🌸 June–Oct
(Achillea millefolium) Daisy Family

- Stems grow to 40cm tall
- Small flowers up to 6mm across are white or pink with an outer ray of five florets and a central disc of cream-white florets. Flowers are grouped in branched, flat-topped to slightly domed clusters
- Leaves are divided into many paired feathery leaflets that are scented when bruised
- Small one-seeded hairless fruits • Insect-pollinated

A hairy perennial herb of grassland, hedgebanks, wasteland, roadside verges and gardens. This plant has been used as a herbal remedy to ease colds.

Wild Angelica   ❀ June–Sept
(Angelica sylvestris) Carrot Family

- Grooved stems are flushed purple and grow to 200cm tall
- Minute pink or white flowers are gathered in stalked clusters forming dome-shaped heads up to 15cm across
- Leaves are divided into 2–3 pairs of pointed, oval and toothed leaflets, with an end leaflet. There are broad sheaths at the base of the stems

An erect hairless perennial found by streams, rivers, lakes, ditches, wet meadows, marshes and fens preferring more calcareous soils. Has been used to produce a yellow dye as well as a flavouring.

Dropwort   ❀ June–Aug
(Filipendula vulgaris) Rose Family

- Branched flowering stems, often flushed red, grow to 50cm tall
- White flowers with a pink-red tinge have six petals and are gathered in leafless branched clusters
- Shiny leaves are divided into many pairs of deeply toothed leaflets

A perennial of roadsides, woodland margins and chalky grasslands. It can sometimes be mistaken for meadowsweet, but has larger flowers that are in fewer numbered clusters and has narrower leaflets.

Cuckooflower   ❀ April–June
(Cardamine pratensis) Cabbage Family

- Grows to 50cm tall
- Pink-white flowers have four petals and yellow anthers and are gathered in loose clusters towards the top of the stem
- Slightly hairy leaves are divided into opposite pairs of rounded leaflets with a larger, kidney-shaped end leaflet
- Fruits are straight, narrow pods
- Insect-pollinated

A perennial herb of damp woodlands, streamsides and damp grassy places such as meadows and some gardens. Also known as Lady's Smock.

Common Centaury
(Centaurium erythraea) Gentian Family

✿ June–Oct

- Square stems up to 50cm tall
- Pink tubular flowers with five spreading petals, grouped together on top of branched stems
- Pale green leaves at base are oval-oblong in a rosette; stem leaves are pointed-oval in opposite pairs
- Fruits are many-seeded capsules
- Self- or insect-pollinated

An annual of sand dunes, cliffs, woodland margins and grasslands around the coast of Britain. It is the most common flower of the Gentian family and has been used in the past to aid digestion.

Common Restharrow
(Ononis repens) Pea Family

✿ June–Sept

- Round hairy stems up are to 80cm long and 30cm high
- Pink flowers are two-lipped, emerging from the leaf base
- Leaves are divided into three pointed, oval, toothed, hairy leaflets
- Fruits are pods that split to release the seeds

A perennial found on sand dunes and grassland around the coasts of Britain, although rarer in the north-west of Scotland. This plant has roots that are said to taste of liquorice.

Lousewort
(Pedicularis sylvatica) Figwort Family

✿ April–July

- Hairless un-branched stems grow to 25cm tall
- Flowers are pink, two-lipped, open, with few flowers held in loose leafy clusters
- Alternating leaves are cut into many opposite and toothed lobes with a similar end lobe
- Fruits are capsules that are held in the remaining flower parts • Insect-pollinated

A perennial with many stems that grow along the ground before rising upwards; a plant of marshes, bogs, damp grassland, damp heaths and woodland flushes. It is partially parasitic, taking its food and water from the roots of other plants.

Red Bartsia
🌸 June–Sept

(Odontites vernus) Figwort Family

- Stems grow up to 50cm tall
- Small pink flowers are two-lipped and in pairs along the leafy stems
- Leaves are in opposite pairs up the stem with few teeth or untoothed
- Fruits are small capsules • Insect-pollinated

Red Bartsia is an annual of wasteland, roadside verges, cultivated and arable land and grassland. This flower can be an abundant weed in corn-fields.

Common Spotted-orchid
🌸 June–Aug

(Dactylorhiza fuchsii) Orchid Family

- Smooth solid stems grow to 60cm tall
- Pale pink flowers with short spurs are streaked and dotted purple and gathered in leafy cone-shaped spikes.
- Leaves at the base of the stem are long, broad and covered in purple spots. Stem leaves are smaller and narrower
- Fruits are twisted capsules • Insect-pollinated

A hairless perennial of grassland, scrub, open woodland and hedgebanks. The flowers can also be found in plain white, or white with purple spots and streaks.

Fragrant Orchid
🌸 June–Aug

(Gymnadenia conopsea) Orchid Family

- Smooth hairless stem grows up to 40cm tall
- Pink, sweetly scented flowers have a curved spur and are gathered in cylindrical spikes
- Unspotted leaves are long, narrow at the base of the plant and folded slightly inwards from the centre. Stem leaves are smaller, in two opposite rows and held close to the stem
- Fruits are twisted capsules
- Insect-pollinated

Fragrant Orchid is a perennial of calcareous grasslands and is chiefly pollinated by moths.

Bog Pimpernel 🌸 June–Aug
(Anagallis tenella) Primrose Family

- Creeping stems grow up to 15cm long
- Flowers are five-lobed and pink with darker veins, grouped in pairs which emerge on long stalks from where the leaves meet the stem
- Leaves are rounded-oval, in opposite pairs and are smaller than the flower
- Fruits are tiny capsules

Bog Pimpernel is a hairless perennial that roots from the underside of each pair of leaves. It is a plant of bogs, fens, wet meadows and other boggy places avoiding shaded areas.

Dove's-foot Crane's-bill 🌸 April–Sept
(Geranium molle) Geranium Family

- Branched hairy stems grow to 10cm tall
- Pink flowers have five notched petals
- Leaves are rounded and cut into 5–7 toothed lobes
- Fruits are hairless, pointed capsules
- Self-pollinated

Dove's-foot Crane's-bill is an annual of dry grassland, sand dunes, wasteland, cultivated and arable land. This plant is similar to other crane's-bills, especially the Small-flowered Crane's-bill, but has smaller hairs on the stems.

Cut-leaved Crane's-bill 🌸 May–Aug
(Geranium dissectum) Geranium Family

- Hairy stems grow to around 60cm tall
- Small pink flowers have five notched petals up to 1cm across
- Leaves are divided into lobes that are again divided into narrow segments
- Fruits are hairy, beaked capsules
- Self-pollinated

Cut-leaved Crane's-bill is an annual of grassy places, cultivated and arable land, hedgebanks, wasteland and roadside verges. It is a similar plant to the Dove's-foot Crane's-bill but differs mainly in the leaves.

Ragged-robin ❀ May–Aug
(Lychnis flos-cuculi) Campion Family

- Grows up to 100cm tall
- Deep pink flowers with five petals that are deeply divided into four narrow lobes
- All leaves are in opposite pairs. Stem leaves are narrow and pointed whilst lower leaves are oblong and larger
- Fruits are capsules • Insect-pollinated

This hairless perennial grows in wet and damp places in meadows, fens, marshes and woodlands. The clove-like scent draws in bumblebees and butterflies by day and moths by night.

Marjoram ❀ July–Sept
(Origanum vulgare) Mint Family

- Branched flushed red stems grow to 80cm tall
- Tiny pink to pinkish-purple flowers are two-lipped and clustered in flat to domed-topped clusters
- Slightly pointed, oval leaves are hairy and in opposite pairs up the stem
- Insect-pollinated

An aromatic perennial herb of rough grasslands, hedgebanks, scrub and roadsides, avoiding more acid soils. It grows throughout Britain, although quite rare in the far north-west of Scotland. Widely used as a flavouring in cooking.

Wild Thyme ❀ May–Aug
(Thymus polytrichus) Mint Family

- Square hairy stems grow to 10cm tall
- Tiny pink to purplish-pink flowers are two-lipped and grouped together in round spikes
- Leaves are spear-shaped and in opposite pairs up the stem
- Fruits are four nutlets held within the remaining flower parts • Insect-pollinated

An aromatic perennial herb found in short chalk grassland, coastal heaths, rocks, and sand dunes of Britain. It is a mat-forming plant with a distinctive smell and hairs only on two opposite sides of the square stem.

Common Vetch
(Vicia sativa) Pea Family

🌸 May–Sept

- Slightly grooved stems grow to 100cm long
- Two-lipped pink or purple flowers are in pairs or solitary along the stem
- Leaves are divided up to eight times into opposite pairs of oblong leaflets that have a tiny bristle at the end. A branched tendril replaces the end leaflet
- Fruits are long flattish pods

A perennial herb that was originally cultivated in Britain as a fodder crop but is now commonly found in meadows, hedgerows, scrub and on the edges of cultivated and arable fields.

Autumn Gentian
(Gentianella amarella) Gentian Family

🌸 July–Sept

- Branched square stems grow to 30cm tall
- Purple to pinkish-purple flowers are bell-shaped with four or five spreading lobes and white hairs within the throat of the flowers
- Leaves are stalkless and oval-pointed in opposite pairs
- Fruits are capsules • Insect-pollinated

A biennial of chalk grassland and sand dunes. The roots have been used in herbal medicine to treat indigestion and stomach ache.

Betony
(Betonica officinalis) Mint Family

🌸 June–Sept

- Square hairy stems grow to 60cm tall
- Two-lipped flowers are reddish-purple and are in whorls around the stem, forming a spike
- Stalked, toothed leaves have heart-shaped bases and are mostly found in a rosette at the base of plant. Stem leaves are in opposite pairs
- Fruits are nutlets • Insect-pollinated

Betony is an un-branched perennial herb of dry grasslands, open woodland, scrub, and heaths throughout most of Britain, although quite rare in the north-east of Scotland.

Common Knapweed   ❀ June–Sept
(Centaurea nigra) Daisy Family

- Grooved branched stems grow to 100cm tall
- Flowers are solitary with reddish-purple florets emerging from a rounded head, covered in brown fringed triangular bracts
- Alternate leaves are oblong or spear-shaped, stalkless further up the stem and stalked below. Some leaves lower down the stem may have opposite pairs of lobes lower down the leaf part
- Fruits are nutlets with a top of short bristles
- Insect-pollinated

Common Knapweed is a hairy perennial of meadows, wasteland, roadsides and grasslands.

Marsh Thistle   ❀ July–Sept
(Cirsium palustre) Daisy Family

- Hairy, spiny, few branched stems grow to 150cm tall
- Many purple florets emerge from egg-shaped heads that are covered in green-purplish bracts and are gathered in compact leafy clusters at the end of the stem
- Leaves are deeply lobed with spiny edges and hairy above • Insect-pollinated

Marsh Thistle is a biennial of marshes, damp grassland and woodlands. This plant can also have white flowers.

Lucerne   ❀ June–Sept
(Medicago Sativa) Pea Family

- Grows up to 90cm tall
- Small purple flowers are two-lipped, closed and gathered in clusters towards the end of the stem
- Leaves are divided into three leaflets; each leaflet is toothed at the end
- Fruits are smooth, spiralled pods
- Insect-pollinated

Lucerne, also known as Alfalfa, is a perennial herb that was originally introduced to Britain for its use as a fodder crop and is now found on wasteland and roadsides throughout Britain.

Devil's-bit Scabious ❀ June–Oct
(Succisa pratensis) Scabious Family

- Grows up to 100cm tall
- Tiny, four-lobed, purplish-blue flowers with long protruding stamens are tightly packed together in domed heads
- Leaves are pointed-oval with a central vein. Stem leaves are in opposite pairs whilst the leaves at the base of the plant are in a rosette
- Fruits are one-seeded • Insect-pollinated

Devil's-bit Scabious is a slightly hairy perennial of marshes, fens, heaths, wet meadows and stream-sides. This plant was used in the past as a cure for scabies.

Tufted Vetch ❀ June–Aug
(Vicia cracca) Pea Family

- Stems grow to 200cm long
- Purplish-blue flowers are two-lipped and grouped in numbers of up to forty on long-stalked one-sided clusters
- Leaves are divided into opposite pairs of narrow, pointed oval leaflets ending with a branched tendril
- Fruits are hairless brown pods

A creeping or climbing perennial of rough grass-lands, scrub, woodland edges and hedgerows.

Bugle ❀ April–July
(Ajuga reptans) Mint Family

- Leafy, square, flowering stems with hairs on two opposite sides growing up to 30cm tall
- Blue tubular flowers with white streaks on the three-lobed lower lip are in whorls around the stem and gathered in a leafy spike
- Shiny leaves are stalked and in a rosette at the base of the plant; stem leaves are unstalked and in opposite pairs
- Fruits are black nutlets • Insect-pollinated

Bugle is a perennial herb with creeping stems that can be found in the more shady parts of damp woodlands, wet meadows and hedgerows.

Common Milkwort ✤ May–Sept
(Polygala vulgaris) Milkwort Family

- Grows to 35cm tall
- Small blue flowers have five petal-like sepals and three small real petals in short-stalked clusters along the stem
- Small pointed leaves are narrowly oval and in alternate pairs up the stem
- Fruits are two-celled capsules

Common Milkwort is a perennial of chalk grasslands and coastal areas. This flower is predominantly blue but can also be found in pink, white or purple.

Skullcap ✤ June–Sept
(Scutellaria galericulata) Mint Family

- Square stems grow to 50cm tall
- Blue, tubular flowers are two-lipped with white markings on lower lip. Flowers are in pairs, growing from where the leaves meet the stem
- Toothed leaves are pointed-oval with a heart-shaped base and are in opposite pairs
- Fruits are nutlets held within the remaining flower parts • Insect-pollinated

Skullcap is a downy perennial herb with creeping underground roots. It is found in damp woodlands, fens and meadows, and by rivers and streams.

Selfheal ✤ June–Sept
(Prunella vulgaris) Mint Family

- Grows up to 25cm tall
- Deep bluish-purple flowers are two-lipped and gathered in dense heads with purplish hairy bracts
- Leaves are stalked, oval and are in opposite pairs up the stem
- Insect-pollinated

Selfheal is a perennial herb with creeping stems growing on grasslands, wasteland, lawns and woodland clearings. The common name of this flower derives from its past use to heal wounds and to stop bleeding.

Brooklime
❀ May–Sept

(Veronica beccabunga) Figwort Family

- Grows to 60cm tall
- Small, deep blue flowers with four petals are grouped in pairs on slender stalks that emerge from where the leaves meet the stem
- Leaves are oval, fleshy, toothed and in opposite pairs
- Fruits are round, flat capsules
- Self- or insect-pollinated

Brooklime is a creeping perennial of marshes, streams, ponds and wet meadows. The young shoots of this flower are edible.

Harebell
❀ July–Oct

*(Campanula rotundifolia)
Bellflower Family*

- Slender flowering stems grow to 40cm tall
- Blue, nodding bell-shaped flowers
- Leaves at base of flower are toothed, long stalked and rounded with a heart-shaped base; stem leaves are narrow, short stalked or stalkless and less toothed.
- Fruits are rounded capsules
- Self- or insect-pollinated

A delicate-looking hairless perennial of fixed sand dunes, dry grasslands, hedgerows and heaths throughout Britain.

Chicory
❀ July–Oct

(Cichorium intybus) Daisy Family

- Hairy, grooved stems grow to 100cm tall
- Circular blue flowers with rays of florets emerge from where the upper leaves meet the stem
- Stem leaves are pointed, spear-shaped and stalkless; leaves at the base of the plant are larger, stalked, deeply lobed and in a rosette
- Fruits are nutlets without hairs
- Insect-pollinated

A perennial herb of wasteland, roadsides and grasslands. Has been used for its medicinal properties and to produce an alternative to coffee.

Germander Speedwell ✿ March–July
(Veronica chamaedrys) Figwort Family

- Flushed red stems with hairs on two opposite sides grow up to 30cm tall
- Four-petalled flowers are blue with a white central eye. Flowers are gathered in stalked spikes
- Toothed leaves are broadly oval-triangular and are in opposite pairs
- Fruits are small hairy capsules

A perennial of grassland, roadsides, hedgebanks, woodlands and wasteland. This flower is the most common of the Speedwells found in Britain, and is pollinated by insects or self-pollinated.

Slender Speedwell ✿ April–June
(Veronica filiformis) Figwort Family

- Slender stems grow up to 20cm tall
- Blue flowers have four petals with white flushed lower petals and a white central eye. Flowers are solitary on long slender stalks emerging from where the leaf stalks meet the stem
- Toothed leaves are blunt, kidney-shaped, long stalked and in opposite pairs
- Fruits are capsules

A mat-forming perennial with creeping underground stems. Not native to Britain, it grows well on grassland, wasteland, gardens, and churchyards, preferring damp grassy places.

Meadow Crane's-bill ✿ June–Sept
(Geranium pratense) Geranium Family

- Sticky, hairy stems grow to 80cm tall
- Violet to blue flowers have five petals with pale veins and are gathered in long stalked pairs
- Leaves are cut into 5–7 cut and toothed lobes. Stem leaves can be stalked or un-stalked
- Fruits are hairy, beaked capsules
- Insect-pollinated

A perennial of grasslands, meadows, roadsides, hedgebanks and other grassy places throughout most of Britain, although rare or absent in the north-west of Scotland.

Field Scabious ✿ July–Sept
(Knautia arvensis) Teasel Family

- Slender hairy flowering stems grow to 100cm
- Flowers of bluish-violet florets massed in flat to slightly domed heads
- Leaves are hairy, in opposite pairs on the stem and are deeply divided into pairs of opposite leaflets with an end leaflet; lower leaves are often unlobed, toothed and larger than stem leaves • Insect-pollinated

A hairy perennial with slender flowering stems growing in open woodlands, grassland, roadsides and hedge banks. This plant has been used in the past to help a variety of skin complaints.

Heath Speedwell ✿ May–Aug
(Veronica officinalis) Figwort Family

- Hairy stems grow to 25cm tall
- Light blue to lilac flowers have four petals with darker streaks and are gathered in dense, short stalked spikes
- Toothed leaves are oval, hairy and in opposite pairs up the stem
- Fruits are small hairy capsules
- Insect-pollinated

Heath Speedwell is a perennial with creeping underground stems of dry grasslands, open woodlands and heaths.

Common Cornsalad ✿ April–June
(Valerianella locusta) Valerian Family

- Branched slender stems grow to 30cm tall
- Tiny pale mauve-lilac flowers have five lobes and are gathered in dense clusters
- Leaves are in opposite pairs and are spoon-shaped lower down the stem and oblong above
- Fruits are swollen nutlets • Self-pollinated

Common Cornsalad is a hairless annual herb of grassland, cultivated and arable land and rocky areas. This plant is also called Lamb's lettuce, and is a popular salad ingredient.

Creeping Thistle ❀ July–Sept
(Cirsium arvense) Daisy Family

- Spineless stems grow to 100cm tall
- Many mauve florets emerge from egg-shaped heads that are covered in scaly, purplish bracts
- Leaves are deeply lobed and edged in sharp spines with upper leaves clasping the stem
- Fruits are one-seeded with a top of white hairs
- Insect-pollinated

Creeping Thistle is the most common of the thistle family and is a flower of roadsides and wasteland. Also a weed in cultivated and arable land.

Marsh-marigold ❀ March–June
(Caltha palustris) Buttercup Family

- Hollow, grooved stems grow to 40cm tall
- Yellow flowers with five shiny petals (actually sepals) and many stamens
- Dark green leaves are toothed and heart-shaped. Lower leaves are stalked, with upper leaves clasping the stem
- Seeds are contained in pods
- Insect-pollinated

Also known as Kingcup, this perennial is the large buttercup-like flower of marshes, fens, woodland flushes, streamsides and wet meadows.

Meadow Buttercup ❀ May–Oct
(Ranunculus acris) Buttercup Family

- Branched, slightly hairy stems grow to 80cm
- Yellow bowl-shaped flowers have five shiny petals and are on smooth stalks
- Toothed leaves are divided into 3–5 deeply divided lobes
- Fruits are nutlets grouped on long stalked heads
- Insect-pollinated

Meadow Buttercup is a tall perennial without creeping stems, found in damp grasslands and meadows. This plant is poisonous to livestock, and is avoided by grazing animals.

Creeping Buttercup ❀ May–Aug
(Ranunculus repens) Buttercup Family

- Grooved stems grow to 60cm tall
- Golden-yellow bowl-shaped flowers are held in branched clusters
- Leaves are divided into three toothed leaflets. Each leaflet is divided again with an end leaflet on a short stalk
- One-seeded fruits are grouped in heads on long stalks
- Insect-pollinated

A fragrant perennial of meadows, damp grassland, wasteland and woodlands throughout Britain.

Bulbous Buttercup ❀ April–June
(Ranunculus bulbosus) Buttercup Family

- Branched flowering stems grow to around 40cm
- Yellow flowers have five shiny petals and five turned-down sepals
- Toothed leaves are divided into three deeply cut lobes
- Fruits are nutlets grouped on long stalked heads
- Insect-pollinated

A hairy perennial of dry well-drained grasslands. It is the earliest of the buttercups to flower, and can be distinguished from the meadow buttercup by its grooved flower stalks and turned-down sepals.

Agrimony ❀ June–Sept
(Agrimonia eupatoria) Rose Family

- Grows up to 100cm tall
- Bright yellow flowers with five petals forming long spikes
- Leaves are divided into opposite pairs of toothed leaflets with smaller pairs of toothed leaflets in between.
- Fruits are grooved and covered with hooked bristles • Self- or insect-pollinated

A hairy perennial of long grasslands, hedgerows and woodland edges. The hooked bristles on the fruit attach to clothes and fur and are carried away, helping to disperse the seeds far and wide.

Silverweed ❀ June–Sept
(Potentilla anserina) Rose Family

- Grows up to 30cm tall
- Solitary dish-shaped yellow flowers have five petals on long leafless stalks
- Leaves are in a rosette at the base of the plant and are divided into pairs of toothed leaflets with a similar end leaflet. All leaves are silvery and hairy underneath
- Fruits are one-seeded • Insect-pollinated

A perennial herb with red creeping stems growing throughout Britain on roadsides, wasteland, damp grassland and some coastal areas on sandy soils.

Tormentil ❀ June–Sept
(Potentilla erecta) Rose Family

- Slender stems grow to around 20cm tall
- Yellow flowers have four petals and are on long stalks that emerge from where upper leaves meet the stem
- Leaves are divided into five toothed leaflets
- Hairless one-seeded fruits are contained in rounded heads

Tormentil is a creeping or erect perennial that at a glance can look like a four petalled buttercup. It is a plant of grasslands, open woodlands, heaths and moors, avoiding chalky or lime-rich soils.

Creeping Cinquefoil ❀ June–Sept
(Potentilla reptans) Rose Family

- Grows to 10cm tall
- Solitary yellow, dish-shaped flowers have five petals and are on long stalks
- Leaves are on long stalks and divided into five seven-toothed leaflets
- Small one-seeded fruits are clustered in round heads • Insect- or self-pollinated

Creeping Cinquefoil is a perennial herb with long creeping stems that are often flushed red. This plant grows well on wasteland, hedge banks, roadsides and dry grasslands.

Common Toadflax ❀ July–Oct
(Linaria vulgaris) Figwort Family

- Grows up to 80cm tall
- Bright yellow flowers are two-lipped with an orange patch on the lower lip and have long straight spurs. Flowers are tightly grouped in spikes
- Narrow leaves are alternate up the stem
- Fruits are oval capsules

Common Toadflax is a perennial of wasteland, hedge banks, cultivated and arable land and some rough grassland. Pollinated by a variety of bees.

Yellow Rattle ❀ May–Aug
(Rhinanthus minor) Figwort Family

- Hairless stems with black spots grow to 50cm
- Yellow two-lipped flowers with two dark teeth on upper lip emerge from a green swollen sack (calyx). Flowers on branched leafy stems
- Toothed leaves are narrow and stalkless in opposite pairs
- Fruits are flat seeds
- Self- or insect-pollinated

An annual of grasslands and meadows with seeds that 'rattle' within the swollen flower parts. This plant is parasitic, gaining its food and water from the roots of other plants.

Common Ragwort ❀ June–Nov
(Senecio jacobaea) Daisy Family

- Grows up to 150cm tall
- Daisy-like flowers are yellow and gathered in branched, flattish-topped clusters
- Leaves are dark green, deeply lobed and slightly toothed. Upper leaves clasp the stem
- Fruits are one-seeded with a top of white hairs
- Insect-pollinated

Ragwort is a biennial or on occasion perennial of rough grasslands, wasteland, roadsides and sand dunes. This plant is toxic to livestock and is therefore pulled extensively in the summer by landowners and conservation groups.

Dandelion   ❀ March–Oct
(Taraxacum officinale) Daisy Family

- Leafless stems grow to 50cm tall
- Solitary yellow flowers consist of rays of strap-shaped florets
- Rosettes of leaves at the base of the plant are cut into opposite pointed lobes, with a larger triangular end lobe
- Fruits are groups of nutlets topped with long white hairs • Wind-pollinated

A perennial of gardens, paths, grassland, dunes and rocky areas. The seeds are grouped together to produce rounded, white fluffy heads. The stems of this plant are often flushed red.

Cat's-ear   ❀ June–Sept
(Hypochoeris radicata) Daisy Family

- Smooth, few-branching stems grow to 40cm
- Flowers are solitary on stems, with rays of strap-shaped florets. Outer florets greyish underneath
- Toothed leaves are hairy, gently lobed and arranged in a rosette around the stem base. Flowering stems have tiny scale-like leaves
- Fruits are one-seeded with white feathery hairs at the top • Insect-pollinated

A perennial herb of dunes, grasslands, meadows and roadsides. Dandelion-like, but has smaller flowers and less fleshy stems. Leaves are edible.

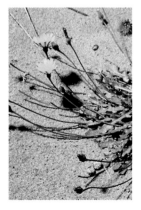

Lesser Hawkbit   ❀ June–Sept
(Leontodon taraxacoides) Daisy Family

- Flowering stems up to 25cm tall
- Yellow flowers are solitary and droop when in bud. Petals are rays of strap-like florets with the outer florets greyish underneath
- Leaves are toothed, hairy, gently lobed and in a rosette around the stem base
- Fruits are one-seeded with white feathery hairs at the top • Insect- or wind-pollinated

A hairy perennial of sandy, well-drained soils of dry grasslands, roadsides, heaths and stable dunes.

Autumn Hawkbit ✿ June–Oct
(Leontodon autumnalis) Daisy Family

- Few-branched stems grow to 50cm tall
- Solitary yellow flowers consist of rays of florets. The underside of flowers are often streaked red
- Dark green, shiny leaves are cut into opposite lobes with a blunt triangular end lobe
- Fruits are heads of nutlets with a top of feathery hairs • Self- or insect-pollinated

A perennial of grasslands, roadsides, gardens and meadows. This flower is one of the many dandelion look-alikes, and is sometimes hard to distinguish from them.

Goat's-beard ✿ June–July
(Tragopogon pratensis) Daisy Family

- Few-branched stems grow to around 80cm
- Solitary yellow flowers with two rays of florets surrounded by up to eight pointed green leaf-like bracts
- Leaves are narrow, alternate, untoothed and slightly clasp the stem
- Fruits are heads of nutlets with a top of feathery white hairs • Self- or insect-pollinated

An annual, biennial or short-lived perennial of grasslands, wasteland and roadsides. The flowers only open in the morning and usually close around midday.

Leafy Hawkweed ✿ June–Oct
(Hieracium umbellatum) Daisy Family

- Branched stems grow to 80cm tall
- Yellow flowers consisting of rays of florets and scale-like bracts that are curved back at the tip. Flowers are in flat-topped clusters
- Stalkless leaves are narrow to spear-shaped, slightly toothed or un-toothed and are mostly alternate
- Fruits are heads of nutlets with a top of white hairs

A hairy perennial of dry grasslands, heaths, roadsides and open woodlands throughout Britain.

Mouse-ear Hawkweed ❀ May–Sept
(Pilosella officinarum) Daisy Family

- Hairy leafless flowering stems grow to 25cm
- Yellow flowers consisting of rays of florets are solitary with red streaks on the underside
- Hairy leaves are spoon-shaped, pale underneath and in a rosette at the base of the plant
- Fruits are heads of dark nutlets with a top of white hairs

Mouse-ear Hawkweed is a perennial with creeping leafy stems and is commonly found on wasteland, heaths, grassland, lawns, walls and grassy banks.

Meadow Vetchling ❀ May–Aug
(Lathyrus pratensis) Pea Family

- Angled stems grow to 120cm tall
- Yellow two-lipped flowers are gathered in long stalked clusters
- Leaves consist of a pair of narrow, spear-shaped leaflets, an end tendril and an opposite pair of arrow-shaped leaf-like structures clasping the stems
- Fruits are pods that turn black when ripe
- Insect-pollinated

A hairless perennial that grows throughout the most of Britain on grasslands, hedgebanks, scrub and woodland borders.

Black Medick ❀ April–Aug
(Medicago lupulina) Pea Family

- Stems up to 60cm long
- Tiny yellow flowers are clustered together forming small rounded heads
- Leaves are short-stalked and divided into three oval leaflets, each leaflet slightly notched
- Fruits are clusters of tiny kidney-shaped pods on long stalks, and turn black when ripe
- Self-pollinated

A hairy annual or short-lived perennial of grasslands, roadsides, shingle beaches, coastal cliffs and sand dunes of Britain. Can be distinguished from yellow clovers by its black fruits.

Hop Trefoil
(Trifolium campestre) Pea Family

❀ June–Sept

- Grows to 30cm tall
- Yellow flowers are rounded heads of tiny florets that turn brown in fruit
- Stalked leaves are slightly toothed and divided into three oval leaflets
- Fruits are one-seeded pods

Hop Trefoil is a hairy annual of short grassland, roadsides, tracks and sand dunes. It is a low-growing flower, like the Lesser Trefoil, but with more florets held in larger flower heads.

Lesser Trefoil
(Trifolium dubium) Pea Family

❀ May–Sept

- Grows up to 10cm tall
- Very tiny yellow flowers clustered in round heads up to 7mm across, on slender stalks
- Leaves are stalked and divided into three oval and toothed leaflets. The end leaflet is on a short stalk
- Fruits are one-seeded brown pods, held in heads of remaining flower parts

A small annual of short grassland, roadsides and hedge banks. Similar to Hop Trefoil, but Lesser Trefoil is smaller and has fewer flowers gathered in the heads.

Common Bird's-foot-trefoil
(Lotus corniculatus) Pea Family

❀ June–Sept

- Grows up to 40cm tall
- Golden yellow flowers are two-lipped and sometimes flushed red or orange. Up to eight flowers are gathered at the top of a long stalk
- Leaves are divided into five pointed-oval leaflets
- Fruits are long pods that are arranged like a 'bird's foot' • Insect-pollinated

Bird's-foot Trefoil is a perennial of short grasslands, roadsides, cliffs and coastal areas of Britain. Has many local names such as 'bacon and eggs' and 'ham and eggs'.

Kidney Vetch
✿ June–Sept
(Anthyllis vulneraria) Pea Family

- Grows up to 30cm tall
- Tiny yellow flowers are clustered in paired rounded heads with a ruff of small leaf-like bracts below. White and woolly at base of flowers
- Leaves are divided into opposite pairs of oval-pointed leaflets with an end leaflet. The green leaves are silvery and hairy underneath
- Fruits are one-seeded flat oval pods held in the flower parts

A soft, hairy perennial of dry grasslands, sand dunes and cliffs, preferring chalky or limestone soils. Can be found in a variety of other colours.

Slender St John's-wort
✿ June–Aug
(Hypericum pulchrum)
St John's-wort Family

- Slender stems, often flushed red, grow to around 80cm tall
- Yellow flowers have five petals and five sepals with black dots, and are gathered in loose branched clusters
- Stalkless oval leaves are in opposite pairs and covered in translucent dots
- Fruits are three-celled capsules

A hairless perennial of grasslands, heaths and open woodlands and scrubland.

Perforate St John's-wort
✿ June–Sept
(Hypericum perforatum)
St John's-wort Family

- Grows up to 90cm tall
- Yellow star-shaped flowers have five petals, often with tiny black dots around the edges, and many stamens
- Leaves are oval or oblong covered with translucent dots and in opposite pairs up the stem • Fruits are capsules

Common or Perforate St John's-wort is a hairless perennial of wasteland, open woodland, roadsides, scrub and grassland. Widely used in herbal medicine. The stems bleed a red sap when cut.

Common Rock-rose ❀ June–Sept
(Helianthemum nummularium)
Rose Family

- Slender stems grow up to 30cm tall
- Yellow flowers are on slender stalks and have five petals
- Oval-oblong leaves are slightly hairy above, hairy-white below and are in opposite pairs
- Fruits are oval capsules that split when ripe
- Insect-pollinated

Rock Rose is a pretty branching shrub of grassland, scrub and rocky ground.

Wild Parsnip ❀ July–Aug
(Pastinaca sativa) Carrot Family

- Grows to 150cm tall
- Tiny yellow flowers are grouped in rays, forming flat-topped heads
- Leaves are divided into oval, toothed leaflets

Wild Parsnip is a branched biennial herb with grooved hollow stems that is commonly found on rough grassland, hedge banks, wasteland and roadside verges. This plant has edible roots that have long been used as a foodstuff. Handling of this plant in the sunlight can irritate the skin and can cause blistering.

Cowslip ❀ April–May
(Primula veris) Primrose Family

- Downy perennial herb growing to 10cm tall
- Scented yellow flowers are gathered in stalked nodding clusters at the top of the stem
- Leaves are toothed with a wrinkled surface and are all at the base of the plant
- Fruits are capsules

The Cowslip is a conspicuous flower of open woodland and hedgebanks, as well as some meadows and grasslands. The flowers of this plant have been used in the past as a sedative and to ease nervous dispositions.

Creeping Jenny ❀ June–Aug
(Lysimachia nummularia) Primrose Family

- Creeping stems grow to 60cm long
- Flowers are tiny, five-lobed, on long stalks arising in pairs from where the leaves meet the stem
- Leaves are small, broad-oval and in opposite pairs
- Fruits are rounded capsules

Creeping Jenny is a perennial of damp grassland and woodlands, found by rivers and streams and in other damp shady areas.

Lady's Bedstraw ❀ July–Sept
(Galium verum) Bedstraw Family

- Square stems grow to 80cm tall
- Scented yellow flowers are tiny with four petals and are clustered along the branched stems
- Leaves are narrow and in whorls of up to twelve around the stem • Insect-pollinated

A perennial herb with creeping stems, growing on sand dunes, coastal heaths and on some grasslands and hedge banks. In the past this flower was commonly used as a stuffing for mattresses and as a flea deterrent.

Marsh Cudweed ❀ July–Sept
(Gnaphalium uliginosum) Daisy Family

- Woolly branched stems grow up to 20cm tall
- Tiny yellowish-brown flowers are in clusters at the top of the stems with a whorl of long narrow leaves below
- Leaves are untoothed and woolly
- Fruits are one-seeded and topped with white hairs • Wind-pollinated

A grey woolly annual favouring damp areas of grassland and marshes; also disturbed, cultivated and arable land. The white hairs on the fruits help to disperse the seeds in the wind.

Wood Sage
✿ June–Sept
(Teucrium scorodonia) Mint Family

- Grows to 60cm tall
- Yellowish-green flowers with only a lower lobed lip are in opposite pairs and grouped in branched spikes
- Toothed leaves have a wrinkled surface, are heart-shaped at the base and in opposite pairs up the stem
- Fruits are nutlets • Insect-pollinated

A downy perennial herb with square stems that are often flushed red. It is a flower of open woodlands, sand dunes, rough grasslands and heaths.

Common Twayblade
✿ May–July
(Listera ovata) Orchid Family

- Grows up to 60cm tall
- Green to yellowish-green flowers have no spurs and are gathered in long spikes
- Leaves are an opposite pair of broad, oval and ribbed leaves towards the base of the stem
- Fruits are twisted capsules
- Insect-pollinated

Common Twayblade is a perennial herb of rough grasslands, open woodlands, scrub and heaths throughout most of Britain, although quite rare in the higher regions of Scotland.

Salad Burnet
✿ May–Aug
(Sanguisorba minor) Rose Family

- Branched, hairless stems grow to 40cm tall
- Flowers are tiny, green, without petals and are tightly clustered into round heads
- Leaves at the base of the plant are stalked and divided into opposite pairs of toothed oval-round leaflets with an end leaflet. Stem leaves are smaller with narrower leaflets
- Wind-pollinated

An erect perennial herb of chalky grasslands throughout Britain. As the name suggests, the leaves of this plant are edible and have been used in salads.

Scarlet Pimpernel
✿ June–Aug

(Anagallis arvensis) Primrose Family

- Angled stems grow to around 40cm long
- Small scarlet flowers are dish-shaped and have five lobes. Flowers are solitary on long slender stalks, which arise in pairs from where the leaves meet the stem
- Leaves are oval, pointed with black dots on the underside and are in opposite pairs
- Fruits are capsules

An annual weed of open grassland, sand dunes and cultivated and arable land, preferring well-drained soils.

Common Sorrel
✿ May–July

(Rumex acetosa) Dock Family

- Branched, grooved stems grow up to 80cm
- Tiny red flowers are in whorls around stem in leafless spikes
- Shiny, arrow-shaped leaves are fleshy and have downward-pointing lobes at the base of the leaves; upper stem leaves clasp the stem
- Fruits are shiny nutlets held in the papery remains of the flower • Wind-pollinated

Common Sorrel is a hairless perennial herb of grassland, roadsides and open woodlands. The male and female flowers are found on separate plants.

Sheep's Sorrel
✿ May–Sept

(Rumex acetosella) Dock Family

- Branched flowering stems grow to 70cm tall
- Flowers are tiny, red and gathered in slender spikes
- Fleshy leaves are oval, pointed with opposite narrow lobes at the base. Stem leaves are on stalks with stem leaves clasping the stem
- Fruits are tiny nutlets
- Wind-pollinated

Sheep's Sorrel is a hairless perennial of short dry grassland, roadside verges, shingle beaches and heaths. The whole of this plant has been used to treat a variety of kidney complaints.

Arable & Waste Land

Common Nettle
123

Greater Plantain 123

Curled Dock
123

Broad-leaved Dock 124

Fat Hen
124

Black-bindweed
124

Japanese Knotweed 125

Corn Spurrey
125

Procumbent Pearlwort 125

Shepherd's-purse 126

Common Chickweed 126

Hairy Bitter-cress 126

Cow Parsley
127

Wild Carrot
127

Sea Mayweed
127

Hemlock
128

Hedge Bindweed 128

White Dead-nettle 128

Alsike Clover 129

Ground-elder 129

White Campion 129

Bladder Campion 130

White Clover 130

Hogweed 130

Star-of-Bethlehem 131

Yarrow 131

Red Bartsia 131

Redshank 132

Common Fumitory 132

Field Bindweed 132

Knotgrass 133

Dove's-foot Crane's-bill 133

Cut-leaved
Crane's-bill 133

Common
Stork's-bill 134

Common
Hemp-nettle 134

Red
Dead-nettle 134

Hedge
Woundwort 135

Indian Balsam
135

Red Clover
135

Wild Onion
136

Common Vetch
136

Spear Thistle
136

Lucerne
137

Winter
Heliotrope 137

Field Madder
137

Opium Poppy
138

Field Forget-
me-not 138

Common Field
Speedwell 138

Chicory
139

Slender
Speedwell 139

Common
Corn-salad 139

Creeping
Thistle 140

Field Pansy
140

Creeping
Buttercup 140

Nipplewort
141

Dandelion
141

Smooth
Sow-thistle 141

Sun Spurge
142

Hedge Mustard
142

Charlock
142

Rape
143

Broom
143

Wild Mignonette
143

Corn Marigold
144

Pineappleweed
144

Tansy
144

Groundsel
145

Colt's-foot
145

Great Mullein
145

Procumbent
Yellow-sorrel 146

Common
Toadflax 146

Silverweed
146

Creeping
Cinquefoil 147

Common
Ragwort 147

Oxford Ragwort
147

Cat's-ear
148

Goat's-beard
148

Mouse-ear
Hawkweed 148

Hop Trefoil
149

Lesser Trefoil
149

ARABLE & WASTE LAND

Common Bird's-foot-trefoil 149   **Perforate St John's-wort** 150   **Wild Parsnip** 150   **Marsh Cudweed** 150

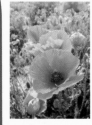

Common Poppy 151   **Scarlet Pimpernel** 151   **Common Sorrel** 151   **Sheep's Sorrel** 152

Mugwort 152

Common Nettle
(Urtica dioica) Nettle Family

✤ June–Aug

- Hairy stems grow to 150cm tall
- Tiny green flowers without petals are grouped together in drooping clusters emerging from the base of the leaf stalks
- Stalked leaves are toothed, pointed with a heart-shaped base
- Wind-pollinated

A hairy perennial that grows well in many habitats such as wasteland, woodlands, hedge banks, roadsides and fens, and by rivers and streams. Both the stem and leaves are covered in stinging hairs that irritate the skin on contact.

Greater Plantain
(Plantago major) Plantain Family

✤ June–Nov

- Leafless flowering stalks grow to 30cm tall
- Tiny greenish flowers are gathered in long dense spikes
- Broad, veined leaves are on long stalks and form a rosette at the base of the stem
- Fruits are small oval capsules • Wind-pollinated

Greater Plantain is a perennial of wasteland, cultivated and arable land and trampled ground. In gardens, it is considered a weed.

Curled Dock
(Rumex crispus) Dock Family

✤ June–Oct

- Slightly grooved stems grow to 120cm tall
- Tiny green flowers are sometimes flushed red and gathered in large numbers around the stems in long spikes
- Long spear-shaped leaves are green, untoothed with crumpled margins
- Fruits are one-seeded in the papery remains of the flower parts • Wind-pollinated

A hairless annual, biennial or perennial of wasteland, roadsides, hedge banks, cultivated and arable land and some coastal areas such as shingle beaches.

Broad-leaved Dock ❀ May–Oct
(Rumex obtusifolius) Dock Family

- Grooved stems grow to 130cm tall
- Tiny green flowers with a red tinge are in whorls around the stem
- Large, heart-shaped leaves; upper stem leaves are smaller and narrower
- Fruits are tiny triangular nutlets
- Wind-pollinated

A hairless perennial herb of hedgebanks, wasteland, cultivated and arable land and by the sides of rivers and streams. This plant is a thriving weed with leaves that are renowned to ease the rash of nettle stings.

Fat Hen ❀ July–Oct
(Chenopodium album) Goosefoot Family

- Grooved stems, often flushed red, growing to 100cm tall
- Tiny green flowers are tightly packed together in long branched clusters
- Leaves are greyish-green to green and can be toothed or un-toothed, stalked or unstalked and vary in shape
- Fruits are nutlets • Wind- or insect-pollinated

Fat-hen is an annual of wasteland and roadsides as well as being a weed of gardens, cultivated and arable land. The leaves of this plant used to be cooked and eaten like greens.

Black-bindweed ❀ July–Oct
(Fallopia convolvulus) Dock Family

- Long slender twining stems grow up to around 100cm long
- Minute greenish-white flowers are gathered in branched loose spikes
- Stalked leaves are triangular or heart-shaped
- Fruits are dull black nutlets

Black-bindweed is a climbing annual weed of wasteland, cultivated and arable land, hedgebanks and gardens. The leaves of this plant are edible and have a slightly sour taste.

Japanese Knotweed ❀ Aug–Oct
(Reynoutria japonica) Dock Family

- Long, hollow stems, often flushed red, grow to 200cm tall
- Tiny, greenish-white flowers are bunched in large numbers along the branched stems
- Leaves are oval, pointed or triangular, growing up to 12cm long • Often not fruiting in Britain

A vigorous hairless perennial with far-reaching underground stems, introduced from Japan in the 1800s as a popular garden plant. It escaped Victorian gardens to become an aggressive weed of wasteland, roadsides, railway banks and stream-sides throughout Britain.

Corn Spurrey ❀ June–Sept
(Spergula arvensis) Campion Family

- Slender stems grow to 30cm tall
- White flowers have five petals and are gathered in branched clusters
- Leaves are blunt, narrow, furrowed underneath and arranged in whorls around the stem
- Fruits are capsules containing tiny narrow-winged seeds • Self- or insect-pollinated

Corn Spurrey is a sticky hairy or hairless annual of dry sandy soils and is a weed of arable and cultivated land. The flowers of this plant only open after midday.

Procumbent Pearlwort ❀ May–Sept
(Sagina procumbens) Campion Family

- Grows to 20cm long
- Tiny white flowers with four petals and larger sepals are solitary on long slender stalks
- Leaves are small, narrow and pointed, and are in opposite pairs or in larger numbers along the stems. A non-flowering leafy rosette is also present at the base of the plant
- Fruits are long-stalked oval capsules
- Self-pollinated

A perennial herb with creeping, rooting flower-ing stems. It is a plant of wasteland, lawns, paths and walls, preferring damp shady areas.

Shepherd's-purse
❀ Jan–Dec

(Capsella bursa-pastoris) Cabbage Family

- Branched stems grow to 40cm tall
- Tiny white flowers (up to 8mm across) have four petals. Flowers are on short stalks and grouped together to form loose spikes
- Leaves at the base of the plant are oblong with almost pointed lobes and are in a rosette. Stem leaves are pointed, narrow and clasp the stem
- Fruits are heart-shaped capsules on long stalks off the stem

An erect annual or biennial of arable and cultivated land, wasteland, roadsides and some gardens.

Common Chickweed
❀ Jan–Dec

(Stellaria media) Campion Family

- Grows to 40cm long
- White flowers with five deeply divided petals in stalked clusters, arising from where the leaves meet the stems
- Stalked and un-stalked leaves are oval, pointed and in opposite pairs
- Fruits are oval capsules • Self-pollinated

Chickweed is a sprawling annual weed with smooth round stems. It is a plant of wasteland, gardens, and cultivated and arable land. At night the leaves cover the flower buds as a means of protection.

Hairy Bitter-cress
❀ March–Nov

(Cardamine hirsuta) Cabbage Family

- Straight hairy stems grow to 25cm tall
- Tiny white flowers (up to 4mm across) have four petals and are sweetly scented. Flowers are grouped together in stalked clusters
- Leaves are stalked and divided into rounded-oval leaflets with an end leaflet. Stem leaves are smaller with narrow leaflets
- Fruits are straight, narrow pods • Self-pollinated

Hairy Bitter-cress is an annual weed of gardens, wasteland, rocks and bare ground.

Cow Parsley
(Anthriscus sylvestris) Carrot Family
❀ April–June

- Grooved hollow stems grow to 150cm tall
- Tiny white flowers have five petals and are gathered in flat-topped to domed umbels
- Fern-like leaves are divided into opposite pairs of pointed leaflets with a similar end leaflet
- Insect-pollinated

Cow Parsley is an erect perennial of rough grassland, hedgerows, woodland edges and roadsides.

Wild Carrot
(Daucus carota) Carrot Family
❀ June–Aug

- Hairy grooved stems grow to 100cm tall
- Tiny white flowers are tightly grouped together to form domed umbels; the central flower of the domed head is usually red. At the base of the flower head is a ruff of deeply divided, narrow leaf-like bracts
- Leaves are stalked and divided into deeply cut fern-like leaflets
- Tiny, oval and hairy one-seeded fruits

A hairy biennial growing on grasslands, roadsides, hedgerows and coastal areas. The leaves smell of carrot when crushed.

Sea Mayweed
(Tripleurospermum maritimum)
Daisy Family
❀ July–Sept

- Hairless branched stems up to 50cm tall
- Flowers have an outer ray of white florets with a central disc of short yellow florets, flowers are up to 4cm across and held in loose clusters.
- Alternate leaves are divided up to three times with each segment divided again into very narrow, almost thread-like parts.

A scentless annual herb of cultivated and arable land, wasteland and roadside verges throughout Britain.

Hemlock ❀ June–July
(Conium maculatum) Carrot Family

- Grooved flowering stems with purple blotches grow to 200cm tall
- Tiny white flowers with five petals are gathered in flat-topped umbels
- Leaves growing to 40cm long are separated into deeply divided fern-like leaflets
- Rounded fruits, one-seeded with wavy ridges

A hairless, unpleasant-smelling biennial of roadside verges, damp wasteland and the sides of streams and rivers throughout Britain, although quite rare in parts of Scotland. The whole of this plant is poisonous and should not be touched.

Hedge Bindweed ❀ July–Sept
(Calystegia sepium) Bindweed Family

- Slender creeping stems grow to 300cm long
- Funnel-shaped flowers are white or white with pink stripes
- Alternate leaves are mainly arrow-shaped and are on long slender stalks
- Fruits are one-seeded capsules held in the remaining flower parts • Insect-pollinated

A slender creeping perennial of hedges, hedgebanks, gardens, wasteland and woodland edges. The long entwining stems from which the leaf and flower stalks emerge bleed a white sap when cut.

White Dead-nettle ❀ April–Nov
(Lamium album) Mint Family

- Square stems grow to 60cm tall
- White flowers are two-lipped, open and in whorls around the leafy stems
- Heart-shaped to spear-shaped toothed leaves are in opposite pairs • Insect-pollinated

White Dead-nettle is a hairy perennial of hedgerows, wasteland, roadsides and some gardens. The leaves of this flower are like those of the Stinging Nettle, but do not have the characteristic stinging hairs.

Alsike Clover
✿ June–Sept

(Trifolium Hybridum) Pea Family

- Slender stems grow to 15cm tall
- Small white florets are tightly grouped together in round heads that are flushed pink below
- Leaves are on long slender stalks and divided into three oval leaflets
- At the base of each leaf stem are two small opposite leaf-like structures (stipules)
- Fruits are pods • Insect-pollinated

Alsike Clover is a perennial herb of wasteland, roadside verges, arable land and some meadows.

Ground-elder
✿ May–July

(Aegopodium podagraria) Carrot Family

- Grooved, hollow stems grow to 100cm tall
- Tiny white flowers are grouped together in slightly rounded umbels
- Leaves are stalked and divided once or twice into three oval, pointed and toothed leaflets
- Fruits are one-seeded and oval

Ground-elder is a hairless perennial with creeping underground stems. It is a plant preferring shady areas of woodland edges, wasteland, hedgerows and roadsides, and is considered a serious weed in gardens.

White Campion
✿ May–Oct

(Silene latifolia) Campion Family

- Hairy stems grow up to 100cm tall
- White scented flowers up to 3cm across have five deeply divided petals
- Flowers are on stalks that emerge from where the leaves meet the stem
- Spear-shaped leaves are in opposite pairs with leaves lower down the stem being larger and broader
- Fruits are oval capsules • Insect-pollinated

A hairy annual, occasionally perennial herb of dry arable and cultivated land, wasteland and hedge banks of Britain.

Bladder Campion
✿ May–Sept
(Silene vulgaris) Campion Family

- Branched stems grow to 90cm tall
- White scented flowers with five deeply divided petals. Each flower has a ribbed, greenish-cream oval sac
- Leaves are oval, pointed, in opposite pairs; those on lower stems are stalked
- Fruits are capsules • Insect-pollinated

A perennial herb of dry grassy places including cultivated and arable land, wasteland, roadsides and hedgerows, preferring sandy calcareous soils. The inflated sac that gives the flower its name is formed from the fused sepals known as the calyx.

White Clover
✿ June–Sept
(Trifolium repens) Pea Family

- Leafless flowering stems grow to 20cm tall
- Tiny white scented florets are grouped together to form characteristic rounded heads
- Leaves are long-stalked and divided into three rounded-oval leaflets. Each leaflet has a white arrow-shaped marking
- Fruits are round heads of brown pods
- Insect-pollinated

Also known as Dutch Clover, this is a hairless perennial with long, creeping, rooting stems. It grows well on grasslands, garden lawns and wasteland. Has been cultivated as a fodder crop.

Hogweed
✿ June–Sept
(Heracleum sphondylium) Carrot Family

- Grooved stems, sometimes flushed red, grow to 200cm tall
- Tiny white or pinkish flowers are tightly grouped together in umbels up to 25cm across
- Leaves are divided into large deeply lobed and toothed leaflets
- Oval, flat and smooth one-seeded fruits

Hogweed is a large biennial of woodlands, hedgerows, roadsides, streamsides and rough grasslands of Britain. The sap is hazardous: it can burn and blister the skin in sunlight.

Star-of-Bethlehem
❀ April–June
(Ornithogalum angustifolum) Lily Family

- Stems grow to 30cm tall
- White cup-shaped to star-like flowers with six petals and a green stripe on the underside
- Long narrow leaves up to 30cm have a white stripe down the centre
- Fruits are capsules

Common Star-of-Bethlehem is a hairless perennial with edible bulbs found in dry grassland, wasteland and roadside verges. The flowers of this pretty plant open at around mid-morning.

Yarrow
❀ June–Oct
(Achillea millefolium) Daisy Family

- Stems grow to 40cm tall
- Small flowers up to 6mm across are white or pink with an outer ray of five florets and a central disc of cream-white florets. Flowers are grouped in branched, flat-topped to slightly domed clusters.
- Leaves are divided into many paired feathery leaflets that are scented when bruised
- Small one-seeded hairless fruits • Insect-pollinated

A hairy perennial herb of grassland, hedgebanks, wasteland, roadside verges and gardens. This plant has been used as a herbal remedy to ease colds.

Red Bartsia
❀ June–Sept
(Odontites vernus) Figwort Family

- Stems grow up to 50cm tall
- Small pink flowers are two-lipped and in pairs along the leafy stems
- Leaves are in opposite pairs up the stem with few teeth or untoothed
- Fruits are small capsules • Insect-pollinated

Red Bartsia is an annual of wasteland, roadside verges, cultivated and arable land and grassland. This flower can be an abundant weed in cornfields.

Redshank
✿ June–Oct

(Polygonum persicaria) Dock Family

- Flushed red stems grow to 80cm tall
- Tiny pink flowers are tightly gathered in a cylindrical spike
- Leaves are alternate and spear-shaped
- Fruits are tiny, black and shiny
- Self- or insect-pollinated

Redshank, also known as Persicaria, is a hairless annual weed of arable and cultivated land, wasteland, and roadsides and by rivers and streams throughout Britain.

Common Fumitory
✿ May–Oct

(Fumaria officinalis) Fumitory Family

- Stems grow to 100cm long
- Tubular pink flowers with dark pink tips are clustered in round-topped spikes
- Leaves are divided up to four times into stalked deeply cut leaflets
- Fruits are round nutlets • Self-pollinated

Common Fumitory is an annual of arable and cultivated land, wasteland, disturbed ground and gardens. The juice of this plant can be an irritant to eyes.

Field Bindweed
✿ June–Sept

(Convolvulus arvensis) Bindweed Family

- Clambering stems grow up to 200cm long
- Funnel-shaped flowers are pink with white stripes, or white or pink stripes
- Green alternate leaves are mostly arrow-shaped and on long stalks
- Fruits are two-celled capsules
- Self- or insect-pollinated

A perennial with creeping underground roots growing well on wasteland, roadsides and some grasslands, and as a weed in arable land and gardens throughout Britain, though quite scarce in the far north of Scotland.

Knotgrass
❀ July–Nov
(Polygonum aviculare) Dock Family

- Branched leafy stems grow to 100cm long
- Tiny pale pink flowers in groups of up to 6 growing where the leaf joins the stem
- Leaves are narrow to spear-shaped, pointed or blunt
- Fruits are dull brown and triangular
- Self-pollinated

A hairless annual of arable and cultivated land, wasteland, roadsides and disturbed ground; also found on some seashores and in gardens. The name derives from the way that the stem swells into 'knots' where the leaves join the stem.

Dove's-foot Crane's-bill ❀ April–Sept
(Geranium molle) Geranium Family

- Branched hairy stems grow to 10cm tall
- Pink flowers have five notched petals
- Leaves are rounded and cut into 5–7 toothed lobes
- Fruits are hairless, pointed capsules
- Self-pollinated

Dove's-foot Crane's-bill is an annual of dry grassland, sand dunes, wasteland, cultivated and arable land. This plant is similar to other crane's-bills, especially the Small-flowered Crane's-bill, but has smaller hairs on the stems.

Cut-leaved Crane's-bill ❀ May–Aug
(Geranium dissectum) Geranium Family

- Hairy stems grow to around 60cm tall
- Small pink flowers have five notched petals up to 1cm across
- Leaves are divided into lobes that are again divided into narrow segments
- Fruits are hairy, beaked capsules
- Self-pollinated

Cut-leaved Crane's-bill is an annual of grassy places, cultivated and arable land, hedgebanks, wasteland and roadside verges. It is a similar plant to the Dove's-foot Crane's-bill but differs mainly in the leaves.

ARABLE & WASTE LAND

Common Stork's-bill ❀ June–Sept
(Erodium cicutarium) Geranium Family

- Hairy flowering stems to 30cm tall
- Pink dish-shaped flowers with five petals; 1–12 loosely grouped flowers on each plant
- Leaves are divided into deeply cut fern-like leaflets
- Fruits are beak-like capsules
- Self- or insect-pollinated

Common Stork's-bill is a hairy annual of sand dunes and cliffs around the coast of Britain, as well as inland on short grasslands with sandy soils.

Common Hemp-nettle ❀ July–Sept
(Galeopsis tetrahit) Mint Family

- Square, hairy stems grow to 100cm tall
- Pink flowers are two-lipped with purplish markings on the lobed lower lip. Flowers arranged in whorls around leafy stems
- Leaves are in opposite pairs, oval and pointed
- Fruits are nutlets held within the remaining flower parts • Self-pollinated

Common Hemp-nettle is a branched, erect annual of arable and cultivated land, hedgerows, woodlands and fens.

Red Dead-nettle ❀ March–Nov
(Lamium purpureum) Mint Family

- Grows to 30cm tall
- Pinkish-purple flowers are two-lipped, in whorls around the leafy stems
- Toothed leaves are stalked, heart-shaped or oval
- Fruits are nutlets • Pollinated by bees

Red Dead-nettle is a downy annual often with purple flushed stems. It is a plant of cultivated and arable land, gardens and wasteland throughout Britain.

Hedge Woundwort ❀ June–Sept
(Stachys sylvatica) Mint Family

- Grows to 100cm tall
- Deep pink-purple flowers have white markings on the lower lip and are in whorls around the stem, forming a flowering spike
- Opposite pairs of leaves are oval, pointed, toothed and stalked • Fruits are nutlets

Hedge Woundwort is a hairy perennial with square stems and a distinctive, rather unpleasant odour. It is a flower of woodland, gardens, hedge banks and wasteland and is pollinated by a variety of bees.

Indian Balsam ❀ July–Oct
(Impatiens glandulifera) Balsam Family

- Flushed red stems grow to 250cm tall
- Pink to purplish-pink flowers are two-lipped with short spurs and are gathered in stalked, loose nodding clusters
- Red-toothed leaves are in whorls of three around the stem
- Fruits are green drooping capsules, which explode to release seeds when ripe
- Insect-pollinated

This annual of riversides, streamsides and other damp shady places was introduced to Britain in the early 19th Century. It has a distinctive scent.

Red Clover ❀ May–Sept
(Trifolium pratense) Pea Family

- Slender hairy stems grow to 60cm tall
- Small pink to purplish-pink florets are tightly grouped together in round heads, with a pair of small leaves directly below each flower head
- Leaves are on long stalks, divided into three oval leaflets with a white arrow-shaped marking
- At the base of each leaf stem are two small leaf-like structures (stipules) • Insect-pollinated

A hairy perennial of grassy places including wastelands, hedgebanks, roadsides and lawns. A variety can also be found on cultivated land as a fodder crop.

Wild Onion
❀ June–July
(Allium vineale) Lily Family

- Grows to 80cm tall
- Pink to purplish-pink flowers grow on stalks from a rounded head of purplish-green, oval bulbs that are partly covered by a paper spathe. The flowers of this plant are not always present
- Long narrow leaves are almost tubular
- Insect-pollinated

A hairless perennial of fixed dunes, arable land, hedgebanks, dry grasslands and roadsides. This plant is also known as Crow Garlic, as it smells strongly of garlic when bruised.

Common Vetch
❀ May–Sept
(Vicia sativa) Pea Family

- Slightly grooved stems grow to 100cm long
- Two-lipped pink or purple flowers are in pairs or solitary along the stem
- Leaves are divided up to eight times into opposite pairs of oblong leaflets that have a tiny bristle at the end. A branched tendril replaces the end leaflet
- Fruits are long flattish pods

A perennial herb that was originally cultivated in Britain as a fodder crop but is now commonly found in meadows, hedgerows, scrub and on the edges of cultivated and arable fields.

Spear Thistle
❀ July–Oct
(Cirsium vulgare) Thistle Family

- Cottony branched stems with spiny wings grow to 150cm tall
- Pink to purple scented flowers are solitary, or few in loose clusters
- Toothed leaves are hairy, deeply lobed and edged with spines
- Heads of one-seeded fruits are topped with white feathered hairs • Insect-pollinated

A biennial of grassland, roadsides, open woodland and hedgebanks throughout Britain. The flowers attract many insects and birds eat the fruits.

Lucerne
(Medicago sativa) Pea Family

- Grows up to 90cm tall
- Small purple flowers are two-lipped, closed and gathered in clusters towards the end of the stem
- Leaves are divided into three leaflets; each leaflet is toothed at the end
- Fruits are smooth, spiralled pods
- Insect-pollinated

Lucerne, also known as Alfalfa, is a perennial herb that was originally introduced to Britain for its use as a fodder crop and is now found on wasteland and roadsides throughout Britain.

Winter Heliotrope
❀ Nov–March
(Petasites fragrans) Daisy Family

- Hairy stems grow up to 25cm tall
- Vanilla-scented, lilac flowers are bell-shaped with an outer ray of florets. Flowers are in a loose spike
- Large toothed leaves are stalked, rounded and kidney-shaped; stem leaves are small and scale-like
- Fruits are one-seeded with a top of white hairs
- Insect-pollinated

A perennial with creeping underground stems found on wasteland, hedge banks, roadsides and by rivers and streams.

Field Madder
❀ May–Nov
(Sherardia arvensis) Bedstraw Family

- Square, hairy stems grow to 30cm tall
- Tiny pinkish-mauve flowers have four petals and are in clusters at the end of the branched stems. Each cluster of flowers has a whorl of small leaves (bracts) just below
- Oval to spear-shaped leaves, with hairs along the edges, are pointed and in whorls of up to six around stem • Insect-pollinated

Field Madder is an annual of wasteland, cultivated land, arable land and some dry grassland areas throughout Britain, although rarer in the far north of England and Scotland.

Opium Poppy ✿ June–Aug
(Papaver somniferum) Poppy Family

- Long, slightly hairy stems grow to 100cm
- Large solitary lilac-mauve flowers have four flimsy petals and a dark centre
- Waxy leaves are grey to bluish-green, slightly toothed and deeply lobed
- Fruits are many-seeded, smooth, oval capsules with a flat top • Wind-pollinated

An annual of cultivated and arable land, wasteland and some gardens, the Opium Poppy is notorious for its white latex that can be used to produce opium, morphine, codeine and other substances. The seeds are also used in cooking.

Field Forget-me-not ✿ April–Sept
(Myosotis arvensis) Borage Family

- Hairy flowering stems grow to 40cm tall
- Pale blue flowers have five petals and a yellow central eye
- Leaves are hairy and mainly stalkless, with one central vein
- Fruits are nutlets which are held within the remaining flower parts

Field Forget-me-not (or Common Forget-me-not) is a hairy annual of disturbed ground, cultivated and arable land, roadsides and some waste ground.

Common Field Speedwell ✿ June–Sept
(Veronica persica) Figwort Family

- Hairy stems grow to around 40cm long
- Small blue flowers have a white central eye and four petals; the lower petal is often white. Each flower is on a slender stalk which emerges from where the leaf meets the stem
- Alternate leaves are short-stalked, toothed, triangular-oval and slightly hairy on the underside
- Fruits are small hairy capsules
- Self- or insect-pollinated

A hairy annual of cultivated and arable land, gardens and wasteland.

Chicory
❀ July–Oct
(Cichorium intybus) Daisy Family

- Hairy, grooved stems grow to 100cm tall
- Circular blue flowers with rays of florets emerge from where the upper leaves meet the stem
- Stem leaves are pointed, spear-shaped and stalkless; leaves at the base of the plant are larger, stalked, deeply lobed and in a rosette
- Fruits are nutlets without hairs
- Insect-pollinated

A perennial herb of wasteland, roadsides and grasslands. Has been used for its medicinal properties and to produce an alternative to coffee.

Slender Speedwell
❀ April–June
(Veronica filiformis) Figwort Family

- Slender stems grow up to 20cm tall
- Blue flowers have four petals with white flushed lower petals and a white central eye. Flowers are solitary on long slender stalks emerging from where the leaf stalks meet the stem
- Toothed leaves are blunt, kidney-shaped, long stalked and in opposite pairs
- Fruits are capsules

A mat-forming perennial with creeping underground stems. Not native to Britain, it grows well on grassland, wasteland, gardens, and churchyards preferring damp grassy places.

Common Cornsalad
❀ April–June
(Valerianella locusta) Valerian Family

- Branched slender stems grow to 30cm tall
- Tiny pale mauve-lilac flowers have five lobes and are gathered in dense clusters
- Leaves are in opposite pairs and are spoon-shaped lower down the stem and oblong above
- Fruits are swollen nutlets • Self-pollinated

Common Cornsalad is a hairless annual herb of grassland, cultivated and arable land and rocky areas. This plant is also called Lamb's lettuce, and is a popular salad ingredient.

ARABLE & WASTE LAND

Creeping Thistle
✿ July–Sept
(Cirsium arvense) Daisy Family

- Spineless stems grow to 100cm tall
- Many mauve florets emerge from egg-shaped heads that are covered in scaly, purplish bracts
- Leaves are deeply lobed and edged in sharp spines with upper leaves clasping the stem
- Fruits are one-seeded with a top of white hairs
- Insect-pollinated

Creeping Thistle is the most common of the thistle family and is a flower of roadsides and wasteland. Also a weed in cultivated and arable land.

Field Pansy
✿ April–Oct
(Viola arvensis) Violet Family

- Flowering stems grow to 30cm tall
- Flowers are pale yellow or cream with a yellow flush on the lower petal, and are solitary on stems
- Leaves are toothed with a pair of deeply divided leaf-like lobes at the base
- Fruits are capsules • Self-pollinated

Field Pansy is a hairless annual of wasteland, cultivated and arable land throughout Britain.

Creeping Buttercup
✿ May–Aug
(Ranunculus repens) Buttercup Family

- Grooved stems grow to 60cm tall
- Golden-yellow bowl-shaped flowers are held in branched clusters
- Leaves are divided into three toothed leaflets. Each leaflet is divided again with an end leaflet on a short stalk
- One-seeded fruits are grouped in heads on long stalks
- Insect-pollinated

A fragrant perennial of meadows, damp grassland, wasteland and woodlands throughout Britain.

Nipplewort
❀ June–Sept
(Lapsana communis) Daisy Family

- Slender branching stems grow up to 80cm tall
- Yellow flowers consist of a ray of florets and are gathered in loose branched clusters
- Toothed leaves at the base of the plant are stalked, oval with opposite lobes below. Stem leaves are smaller, stalkless and without lobes
- Fruits are hairless, ribbed nutlets
- Insect-pollinated

An annual of hedgerows, wasteland, walls, woodland edges and some gardens throughout Britain. The young leaves of this plant are edible.

Dandelion
❀ March–Oct
(Taraxacum officinale) Daisy Family

- Leafless stems grow to 50cm tall
- Solitary yellow flowers consist of rays of strap-shaped florets
- Rosettes of leaves at the base of the plant are cut into opposite pointed lobes, with a larger triangular end lobe
- Fruits are groups of nutlets topped with long white hairs • Wind-pollinated

A perennial of gardens, paths, grassland, dunes and rocky areas. The seeds are grouped together to produce rounded, white fluffy heads. The stems of this plant are often flushed red.

Smooth Sow-thistle
❀ June–Oct
(Sonchus oleraceus) Daisy Family

- Smooth branched flowering stems grow to 150cm
- Pale yellow flowers consisting of rays of florets are in branched clusters
- Alternate leaves are deeply lobed and sharply toothed; stem leaves clasp the stem
- Fruits are yellow nutlets topped with hairs
- Insect-pollinated

Smooth Sow-thistle is an annual of wasteland, open woodlands and hedgebanks, and is a weed of gardens, cultivated and arable land. In the past this plant has been eaten as a vegetable.

ARABLE & WASTE LAND

Sun Spurge
🌼 May–Oct
(Euphorbia helioscopia) Spurge Family

- Hairless branched stem grows to 50cm tall
- Minute yellowish flowers enclosed in a cup-like structure. Green, oval glands are also present amongst the flowers. Flower parts are surrounded by five greenish yellow, toothed, leaf-like structures and are grouped in umbel-like clusters
- Leaves are blunt and toothed at the end
- Fruits are smooth capsules

An annual of wasteland, roadsides and arable land. The juice of this plant has been applied as a cure for warts.

Hedge Mustard
🌼 May–Sept
(Sisymbrium officinale) Cabbage Family

- Branched stems grow to 100cm tall
- Tiny yellow flowers have four petals and are gathered in short stalked clusters
- Leaves are deeply cut into opposite toothed lobes with a larger end lobe. Stem leaves are smaller than those at the base of the plant
- Fruits are pods that lie close to the stems
- Self-pollinated

An annual or biennial herb of hedge banks, wasteland and roadsides. The plant smells of mustard when disturbed and crushed underfoot.

Charlock
🌼 May–Aug
(Sinapis arvensis) Cabbage Family

- Hairy stems grow to 60cm tall
- Small yellow flowers with four petals gathered in loose clusters
- Leaves at the base of the plant are toothed, oval to spear-shaped with a pair of opposite lobes below. Upper leaves are narrower, untoothed and unlobed
- Fruits are beaked pods • Insect-pollinated

Also commonly called Wild Mustard, this is a hairy annual of roadsides, wasteland and arable and cultivated ground. The leaves of this plant are edible.

Rape

🌸 May–Aug

(Brassica napus) Cabbage Family

- Stems grow up to 120cm tall
- Pale yellow flowers with four petals gathered in loose domed clusters
- Greyish-green leaves are lobed and stalked on the lower stems; upper leaves are smaller, without lobes, clasping the stem
- Fruits are beaked pods • Insect-pollinated

Rape is a biennial or annual of wasteland, roadsides and cultivated and arable ground. A variant of this species is widely cultivated in Britain for its oil.

Broom

🌸 May–June

(Cytisus scoparius) Pea Family

- Angled stems grow up to 300cm tall
- Scented golden yellow flowers are two-lipped and gathered along the branched leafy stems
- Small leaves (smaller than flowers) are short stalked and divided into three leaflets
- Fruits are flattish, black, hairy pods
- Insect-pollinated

Broom is a shrub without spines (like Gorse) of wasteland, roadsides, railway banks, scrubland and heaths throughout Britain. The pods of this flower burst when ripe, helping dispersal.

Wild Mignonette

🌸 June–Sept

(Reseda lutea) Mignonette Family

- Branched, grooved stems grow to 80cm tall
- Tiny yellow flowers are gathered in long spikes
- Leaves at the base of the plant are in a rosette; stem leaves are deeply divided up to three times into narrow opposite lobes and an end lobe.
- Fruits are open-topped capsules containing tiny black seeds • Self- or insect-pollinated

A biennial or perennial that grows well on the chalky soils of grassland, wasteland and disturbed ground throughout Britain, although this plant can be quite rare or absent from parts of Scotland.

Corn Marigold ❀ June–Aug
(Chrysanthemum segetum) Daisy Family

- Grows to 50cm tall
- Solitary, golden yellow flowers have short disc florets and an outer ray of strap-shaped florets
- Fleshy green leaves are deeply toothed and clasp the stem; upper leaves are smaller and less deeply toothed
- Fruits are hairless nutlets • Insect-pollinated

Corn Marigold is a hairless annual that grows well on the sandy soils of wasteland and arable and cultivated land.

Pineappleweed ❀ May–Oct
(Matricaria discoidea) Daisy Family

- Grows to 40cm tall
- Flowers are rounded to cone-shaped heads of tiny yellow florets that are without an outer ray of florets
- Alternate leaves are divided into feathery segments

Pineappleweed is an annual of tracks, roadsides, waste ground and found by cultivated land. It is resistant to trampling, and smells of pineapple when crushed.

Tansy ❀ July–Sept
(Tanacetum vulgare) Daisy Family

- Grows up to 150cm tall
- Scented flowers are button-shaped, gathered in flat-topped to slightly rounded clusters
- Leaves are toothed and in alternate pairs. Each leaf is deeply cut into opposite lobes with a similar end lobe
- Fruits are nutlets without any hairs
- Insect-pollinated

A hairless perennial herb of wasteland, hedges, roadsides; also found by rivers and streams. Its leaves have been used in a variety of herbal remedies to treat worms, gout and fever.

Groundsel
✿ March–Dec

(Senecio vulgaris) Daisy

- Grows up to 40cm tall
- Yellow flowers with no outer ray of florets are grouped in loose branched clusters
- Leaves are irregularly lobed and toothed with hairs on the underside; leaves can be opposite or alternate, and usually clasp the stem
- Fruits are nutlets with a top of white hairs.
- Self- and wind-pollinated

Groundsel is a hairy annual weed of cultivated and arable land, wasteland, gardens and sand dunes.

Colt's-foot
✿ Feb–April

(Tussilago farfara) Daisy Family

- Scaly flowering stems grow to 30cm tall
- Solitary flowers are yellow and consist of disc florets and an outer ray of many narrow florets
- Large stalked leaves are heart-shaped and toothed with silvery-white hairs below
- Fruits are nutlets with a top of white hairs
- Insect-pollinated

A perennial herb of wasteland, roadsides, sand dunes and of the banks besides rivers and streams. The flower of the Colt's-foot closes at night and in dim weather; the leaves appear after flowering.

Great Mullein
✿ June–Aug

(Verbascum thapsus) Figwort Family

- Thick woolly stems grow to 200cm tall
- Yellow flowers with five petals are densely grouped together in a long spike
- Large woolly greyish-green leaves are in a basal rosette, short-stalked, and alternate on the stem
- Fruits are oval capsules
- Self- or insect-pollinated

Great Mullein is a conspicuous biennial of scrub, woodlands, hedge banks and wasteland. The thick hairs of this plant help prevent moisture loss and attacks by insects.

ARABLE & WASTE LAND

Procumbent Yellow-sorrel
❀ May–Sept
(Oxalis corniculata) Wood-sorrel Family

- Slender stems grow to 50cm tall
- Yellow flowers with five petals are gathered in slender-stalked clusters
- Leaves are on long slender stalks and divided into three heart-shaped leaflets
- Fruits are stalked, downy capsules

Procumbent Yellow-sorrel is a creeping and ascending perennial weed of roadsides, wasteland and gardens throughout England. This pretty non-native weed is rare or absent from most of Scotland.

Common Toadflax
❀ July–Oct
(Linaria vulgaris) Figwort Family

- Grows up to 80cm tall
- Bright yellow flowers are two-lipped with an orange patch on the lower lip and have long straight spurs. Flowers are tightly grouped in spikes
- Narrow leaves are alternate up the stem
- Fruits are oval capsules

Common Toadflax is a perennial of wasteland, hedge banks, cultivated and arable land and some rough grassland. Pollinated by a variety of bees.

Silverweed
❀ June–Sept
(Potentilla anserina) Rose Family

- Grows up to 30cm tall
- Solitary dish-shaped yellow flowers have five petals on long leafless stalks
- Leaves are in a rosette at the base of the plant and are divided into pairs of toothed leaflets with a similar end leaflet. All leaves are silvery and hairy underneath
- Fruits are one-seeded • Insect-pollinated

A perennial herb with red creeping stems growing throughout Britain on roadsides, wasteland, damp grassland and some coastal areas on sandy soils.

Creeping Cinquefoil ❀ June–Sept
(Potentilla reptans) Rose Family

- Grows to 10cm tall
- Solitary yellow, dish-shaped flowers have five petals and are on long stalks
- Leaves are on long stalks and divided into five seven-toothed leaflets
- Small one-seeded fruits are clustered in round heads • Insect- or self-pollinated

Creeping Cinquefoil is a perennial herb with long creeping stems that are often flushed red. This plant grows well on wasteland, hedge banks, roadsides and dry grasslands.

Common Ragwort ❀ June–Nov
(Senecio jacobaea) Daisy Family

- Grows up to 150cm tall
- Daisy-like flowers are yellow and gathered in branched, flattish-topped clusters
- Leaves are dark green, deeply lobed and slightly toothed. Upper leaves clasp the stem
- Fruits are one-seeded with a top of white hairs
- Insect-pollinated

Ragwort is a biennial or on occasion perennial of rough grasslands, wasteland, roadsides and sand dunes. This plant is toxic to livestock and is therefore pulled extensively in the summer by landowners and conservation groups.

Oxford Ragwort ❀ May–Dec
(Senecio squalidus) Daisy Family

- Slightly grooved flowering stems grow to 60cm
- Yellow flowers have a disc and outer ray of florets and are gathered in loose-branched clusters.
- Dark green leaves are cut into narrow toothed lobes; upper stem leaves clasp the stem
- Fruits are nutlets • Wind-pollinated

Oxford Ragwort is an annual found on wasteland and walls, and alongside railways. This plant escaped from the Oxford botanical gardens in the late 1700s, from where it has spread readily ever since.

Cat's-ear   ✿ June–Sept
(Hypochoeris radicata) Daisy Family

- Smooth, few-branching stems grow to 40cm
- Flowers are solitary on stems, with rays of strap-shaped florets. Outer florets greyish underneath
- Toothed leaves are hairy, gently lobed and arranged in a rosette around the stem base. Flowering stems have tiny scale-like leaves
- Fruits are one-seeded with white feathery hairs at the top • Insect-pollinated

A perennial herb of dunes, grasslands, meadows and roadsides. Dandelion-like, but has smaller flowers and less fleshy stems. Leaves are edible.

Goat's-beard   ✿ June–July
(Tragopogon pratensis) Daisy Family

- Few-branched stems grow to around 80cm
- Solitary yellow flowers with two rays of florets surrounded by up to eight pointed green leaf-like bracts
- Leaves are narrow, alternate, untoothed and slightly clasp the stem
- Fruits are heads of nutlets with a top of feathery white hairs • Self- or insect-pollinated

An annual, biennial or short-lived perennial of grasslands, wasteland and roadsides. The flowers only open in the morning and usually close around midday.

Mouse-ear Hawkweed   ✿ May–Sept
(Pilosella officinarum) Daisy Family

- Hairy leafless flowering stems grow to 25cm
- Yellow flowers consisting of rays of florets are solitary with red streaks on the underside
- Hairy leaves are spoon-shaped, pale underneath and in a rosette at the base of the plant
- Fruits are heads of dark nutlets with a top of white hairs

Mouse-ear Hawkweed is a perennial with creeping leafy stems and is commonly found on wasteland, heaths, grassland, lawns, walls and grassy banks.

Hop Trefoil
❀ June–Sept
(Trifolium campestre) Pea Family

- Grows to 30cm tall
- Yellow flowers are rounded heads of tiny florets that turn brown in fruit
- Stalked leaves are slightly toothed and divided into three oval leaflets
- Fruits are one-seeded pods

Hop Trefoil is a hairy annual of short grassland, roadsides, tracks and sand dunes. It is a low-growing flower, like the Lesser Trefoil, but with more florets held in larger flower heads.

Lesser Trefoil
❀ May–Sept
(Trifolium dubium) Pea Family

- Grows up to 10cm tall
- Very tiny yellow flowers clustered in round heads up to 7mm across, on slender stalks
- Leaves are stalked and divided into three oval and toothed leaflets. The end leaflet is on a short stalk
- Fruits are one-seeded brown pods, held in heads of remaining flower parts

A small annual of short grassland, roadsides and hedge banks. Similar to Hop Trefoil, but Lesser Trefoil is smaller and has fewer flowers gathered in the heads.

Common Bird's-foot-trefoil
❀ June–Sept
(Lotus corniculatus) Pea Family

- Grows up to 40cm tall
- Golden yellow flowers are two-lipped and sometimes flushed red or orange. Up to eight flowers are gathered at the top of a long stalk
- Leaves are divided into five pointed-oval leaflets
- Fruits are long pods that are arranged like a 'bird's foot' • Insect-pollinated

Bird's-foot Trefoil is a perennial of short grass-lands, roadsides, cliffs and coastal areas of Britain. Has many local names such as 'bacon and eggs' and 'ham and eggs'.

Perforate St John's-wort ✾ June–Sept
(Hypericum perforatum)
St John's-wort Family

- Grows up to 90cm tall
- Yellow star-shaped flowers have five petals, often with tiny black dots around the edges, and many stamens
- Leaves are oval or oblong covered with translucent dots and in opposite pairs up the stem • Fruits are capsules

Common or Perforate St John's-wort is a hairless perennial of wasteland, open woodland, roadsides, scrub and grassland. Widely used in herbal medicine. The stems bleed a red sap when cut.

Wild Parsnip ✾ July–Aug
(Pastinaca sativa) Carrot Family

- Grows to 150cm tall
- Tiny yellow flowers are grouped in rays, forming flat-topped heads
- Leaves are divided into oval, toothed leaflets

Wild Parsnip is a branched biennial herb with grooved hollow stems that is commonly found on rough grassland, hedge banks, wasteland and roadside verges. This plant has edible roots that have long been used as a foodstuff. Handling of this plant in the sunlight can irritate the skin and can cause blistering.

Marsh Cudweed ✾ July–Sept
(Gnaphalium uliginosum) Daisy Family

- Woolly branched stems grow up to 20cm tall
- Tiny yellowish-brown flowers are in clusters at the top of the stems with a whorl of long narrow leaves below
- Leaves are untoothed and woolly
- Fruits are one-seeded and topped with white hairs • Wind-pollinated

A grey woolly annual favouring damp areas of grassland and marshes; also disturbed, cultivated and arable land. The white hairs on the fruits help to disperse the seeds in the wind.

Common Poppy ❀ June–Aug
(Papaver rhoeas) Poppy Family

- Hairy flowering stems grow to 60cm tall
- Large flowers are red with dark patches in the centre and four flimsy petals
- Leaves are greyish green and divided into opposite pairs of narrow slightly toothed lobes
- Fruits are large rounded capsules

Common Poppy is a highly recognisable annual of arable land, wasteland, roadsides and disturbed ground. The capsules have holes in the top where the small seeds are dispersed in the wind.

Scarlet Pimpernel ❀ June–Aug
(Anagallis arvensis) Primrose Family

- Angled stems grow to around 40cm long
- Small scarlet flowers are dish-shaped and have five lobes. Flowers are solitary on long slender stalks, which arise in pairs from where the leaves meet the stem
- Leaves are oval, pointed with black dots on the underside and are in opposite pairs
- Fruits are capsules

An annual weed of open grassland, sand dunes and cultivated and arable land, preferring well-drained soils.

Common Sorrel ❀ May–July
(Rumex acetosa) Dock Family

- Branched, grooved stems grow up to 80cm
- Tiny red flowers are in whorls around stem in leafless spikes
- Shiny, arrow-shaped leaves are fleshy and have downward-pointing lobes at the base of the leaves; upper stem leaves clasp the stem
- Fruits are shiny nutlets held in the papery remains of the flower • Wind-pollinated

Common Sorrel is a hairless perennial herb of grassland, roadsides and open woodlands. The male and female flowers are found on separate plants.

Sheep's Sorrel
※ May–Sept
(Rumex acetosella) Dock Family

- Branched flowering stems grow to 70cm tall
- Flowers are tiny, red and gathered in slender spikes
- Fleshy leaves are oval, pointed with opposite narrow lobes at the base. Stem leaves are on stalks with stem leaves clasping the stem
- Fruits are tiny nutlets
- Wind-pollinated

Sheep's Sorrel is a hairless perennial of short dry grassland, roadside verges, shingle beaches and heaths. The whole of this plant has been used to treat a variety of kidney complaints.

Mugwort
※ July–Sept
(Artemisia vulgaris) Daisy Family

- Grooved stems, flushed red, grow to 150cm
- Tiny oval flowers are topped with reddish-brown florets and are in branched clusters
- Leaves are deeply divided into narrow lobes which are white and woolly underneath; upper stem leaves are unstalked and less divided than lower stem leaves
- Fruits are hairless nutlets • Wind-pollinated

Mugwort is a perennial of wasteland, roadsides and hedge banks throughout Britain. Has been used in the past to flavour drinks.

Gardens, Paths & Walls

Daisy 157

Feverfew 157

Common Chickweed 157

Enchanter's-nightshade 158

Hairy Bitter-cress 158

Cow Parsley 158

Ground-elder 159

Field Bindweed 159

Sticky Mouse-ear 159

Lesser Stitchwort 160

White Clover 160

Red Clover 160

Hedge Woundwort 161

Red Dead-nettle 161

Herb-robert 161

Ivy-leaved Toadflax 162

Cuckooflower
162

**Slender
Speedwell** 162

**Creeping
Buttercup** 163

Wallflower
163

**Procumbent
Yellow-sorrel** 163

Wall Lettuce
164

Dandelion
164

Cat's-ear
164

**Autumn
Hawkbit** 165

**Mouse-ear
Hawkweed** 165

Hop Trefoil
165

Lesser Trefoil
166

Daisy 🌸 March–Dec
(Bellis perennis) Daisy Family

- Hairy, leafless, flowering stems grow to 15cm tall
- Solitary flowers with a yellow central disc of florets and an outer ray of white florets that are often tinged red underneath
- Leaves are short-stalked, spoon-shaped and are gathered in a low-lying rosette at the base of the plant
- Fruits are heads of downy nutlets

Daisy is a hairy perennial herb of garden lawns and other places with short grass throughout Britain. The long-stemmed flowers are picked by children to make daisy chains.

Feverfew 🌸 July–Sept
(Chrysanthemum parthenium) Daisy Family

- Grows to 60cm tall
- Flowers have a central disc of yellow florets with an outer ray of white florets. Flowers are held in branched, flat-topped clusters
- Light green leaves are cut into bluntly toothed segments; lower stem leaves are on long stalks
- Fruits are hairless, ribbed nutlets

Feverfew is a biennial or perennial herb with branched stems and a strong bitter aroma. It is a wild flower of wasteland, roadsides, hedgerows and gardens.

Common Chickweed 🌸 Jan–Dec
(Stellaria media) Campion Family

- Grows to 40cm long
- White flowers with five deeply divided petals in stalked clusters, arising from where the leaves meet the stems
- Stalked and un-stalked leaves are oval, pointed and in opposite pairs
- Fruits are oval capsules • Self-pollinated

Chickweed is a sprawling annual weed with smooth round stems. It is a plant of wasteland, gardens, and cultivated and arable land. At night the leaves cover the flower buds as a means of protection.

GARDENS, PATHS & WALLS

Enchanter's-nightshade ❀ June–Aug
(Circaea lutetiana) Willowherb Family

- Slightly downy stems grow to 70cm tall
- Tiny white flowers have two divided petals and are gathered in long, leafless spikes
- Stalked leaves are heart-shaped or spear-shaped and in opposite pairs
- Tiny cotton-bud-shaped fruits
- Insect-pollinated

An erect perennial of hedgerows, woodlands and shaded gardens. Animals and people disperse the seeds of this plant as the white, hooked bristles of the fruits easily attach to fur or clothing and are carried away.

Hairy Bitter-cress ❀ March–Nov
(Cardamine hirsuta) Cabbage Family

- Straight hairy stems grow to 25cm tall
- Tiny white flowers (up to 4mm across) have four petals and are sweetly scented. Flowers are grouped together in stalked clusters
- Leaves are stalked and divided into rounded-oval leaflets with an end leaflet. Stem leaves are smaller with narrow leaflets
- Fruits are straight, narrow pods • Self-pollinated

Hairy Bitter-cress is an annual weed of gardens, wasteland, rocks and bare ground.

Cow Parsley ❀ April–June
(Anthriscus sylvestris) Carrot Family

- Grooved hollow stems grow to 150cm tall
- Tiny white flowers have five petals and are gathered in flat-topped to domed umbels
- Fern-like leaves are divided into opposite pairs of pointed leaflets with a similar end leaflet
- Insect-pollinated

Cow Parsley is an erect perennial of rough grassland, hedgerows, woodland edges and roadsides.

Ground-elder ✤ May–July
(Aegopodium podagraria) Carrot Family

- Grooved, hollow stems grow to 100cm tall
- Tiny white flowers are grouped together in slightly rounded umbels
- Leaves are stalked and divided once or twice into three oval, pointed and toothed leaflets
- Fruits are one-seeded and oval

Ground-elder is a hairless perennial with creeping underground stems. It is a plant preferring shady areas of woodland edges, wasteland, hedgerows and roadsides, and is considered a serious weed in gardens.

Field Bindweed ✤ June–Sept
(Convolvulus arvensis) Bindweed Family

- Clambering stems grow up to 200cm long
- Funnel-shaped flowers are pink with white stripes, or white or pink stripes
- Green alternate leaves are mostly arrow-shaped and on long stalks
- Fruits are two-celled capsules
- Self- or insect-pollinated

A perennial with creeping underground roots growing well on wasteland, roadsides and some grasslands, and as a weed in arable land and gardens throughout Britain, though quite scarce in the far north of Scotland.

Sticky Mouse-ear ✤ April–Sept
(Cerastium glomeratum) Campion Family

- Grows to 20cm tall
- White flowers with five deeply cut petals in a dense domed clusters at the end of the stems
- Sticky-hairy leaves are oval, stalkless and in opposite pairs
- Fruits are hairy capsules • Self-pollinated

Sticky Mouse-ear is a sticky, hairy annual herb with branching stems and grows on wasteland, walls, hedge banks, cultivated and arable land, as well as some coastal areas.

Lesser Stitchwort
❀ May–Aug

(Stellaria graminea) Campion Family

- Grows to 60cm tall
- White flowers with five deeply divided petals, few flowers are gathered in loose stalked clusters
- Small, pointed leaves are narrow, spear-shaped, and are in opposite pairs
- Fruits are round capsules • Insect-pollinated

A hairless perennial herb with slender square stems. It is a wild flower of grassland, hedgebanks, heaths and woodland clearings, preferring acid ground. It is a similar plant to Greater Stitchwort but has smaller flowers, more deeply divided petals and smaller leaves.

White Clover
❀ June–Sept

(Trifolium repens) Pea Family

- Leafless flowering stems grow to 20cm tall
- Tiny white scented florets are grouped together to form characteristic rounded heads
- Leaves are long-stalked and divided into three rounded-oval leaflets. Each leaflet has a white arrow-shaped marking
- Fruits are round heads of brown pods
- Insect-pollinated

Also known as Dutch Clover, this is a hairless perennial with long, creeping, rooting stems. It grows well on grasslands, garden lawns and wasteland. Has been cultivated as a fodder crop.

Red Clover
❀ May–Sept

(Trifolium pratense) Pea Family

- Slender hairy stems grow to 60cm tall
- Small pink to purplish-pink florets are tightly grouped together in round heads, with a pair of small leaves directly below each flower head.
- Leaves are on long stalks, divided into three oval leaflets with a white arrow-shaped marking
- At the base of each leaf stem are two small leaf-like structures (stipules) • Insect-pollinated

A hairy perennial of grassy places including wastelands, hedgebanks, roadsides and lawns. A variety can also be found on cultivated land as a fodder crop.

GARDENS, PATHS & WALLS

Hedge Woundwort
🌼 June–Sept

(Stachys sylvatica) Mint Family

- Grows to 100cm tall
- Deep pink-purple flowers have white markings on the lower lip and are in whorls around the stem, forming a flowering spike
- Opposite pairs of leaves are oval, pointed, toothed and stalked • Fruits are nutlets

Hedge Woundwort is a hairy perennial with square stems and a distinctive, rather unpleasant odour. It is a flower of woodland, gardens, hedge banks and wasteland and is pollinated by a variety of bees.

Red Dead-nettle
🌼 March–Nov

(Lamium purpureum) Mint Family

- Grows to 30cm tall
- Pinkish-purple flowers are two-lipped, in whorls around the leafy stems
- Toothed leaves are stalked, heart-shaped or oval
- Fruits are nutlets • Pollinated by bees

Red Dead-nettle is a downy annual often with purple flushed stems. It is a plant of cultivated and arable land, gardens and wasteland throughout Britain.

Herb-robert
🌼 May–Sept

(Geranium robertianum) Gentian Family

- Flushed hairy stems grow to 50cm tall
- Pink flowers have five petals with pale streaks on paired branches off the stem
- Bright green leaves are divided into deeply cut leaflets
- Fruits are beak-like capsules

Herb-robert is a strong-smelling, hairy annual herb of woodlands, hedgerows, shaded gardens and shingle beaches of Britain. It can be mistaken for another flower, Little-Robin, although this has smaller flowers and yellow anthers.

Ivy-leaved Toadflax ❀ May–Sept
(Cymbalaria muralis) Figwort Family

- Slender flushed red stems grow to 60cm
- Tiny two-lipped flowers are lilac with white and yellow patches, and are solitary on long slender stems arising from where the leaf stalk meets the stem
- Long stalked leaves are kidney-shaped or ivy-like with around five triangular lobes
- Fruits are small, stalked capsules
- Insect-pollinated

A non-native hairless perennial herb of walls, wasteland and rocky habitats. It is a pretty little flower that often goes unnoticed by passers-by.

Cuckooflower ❀ April–June
(Cardamine pratensis) Cabbage Family

- Grows to 50cm tall
- Pink-white flowers have four petals and yellow anthers and are gathered in loose clusters towards the top of the stem
- Slightly hairy leaves are divided into opposite pairs of rounded leaflets with a larger, kidney-shaped end leaflet
- Fruits are straight, narrow pods
- Insect-pollinated

A perennial herb of damp woodlands, streamsides and damp grassy places such as meadows and some gardens. Also known as Lady's Smock.

Slender Speedwell ❀ April–June
(Veronica filiformis) Figwort Family

- Slender stems grow up to 20cm tall
- Blue flowers have four petals with white flushed lower petals and a white central eye. Flowers are solitary on long slender stalks emerging from where the leaf stalks meet the stem
- Toothed leaves are blunt, kidney-shaped, long stalked and in opposite pairs
- Fruits are capsules

A mat-forming perennial with creeping underground stems. Not native to Britain, it grows well on grassland, wasteland, gardens, and churchyards preferring damp grassy places.

Creeping Buttercup ❀ May–Aug

(Ranunculus repens) Buttercup Family

- Grooved stems grow to 60cm tall
- Golden-yellow bowl-shaped flowers are held in branched clusters
- Leaves are divided into three toothed leaflets. Each leaflet is divided again with an end leaflet on a short stalk
- One-seeded fruits are grouped in heads on long stalks
- Insect-pollinated

A fragrant perennial of meadows, damp grassland, wasteland and woodlands throughout Britain.

Wallflower ❀ April–June

(Erysimum cheiri) Cabbage Family

- Branched stems grows to 60cm tall
- Scented yellow flowers, sometimes flushed with orange, are in short-stalked clusters
- Spear-shaped leaves are untoothed with flat branching hairs
- Fruits are long, hairy, flattish pods
- Insect-pollinated

A non-native biennial or perennial shrub. This fragrant plant was introduced to Britain's gardens around 300 years ago and has since escaped to become a common sight on rocky ground, cliffs and old walls.

Procumbent Yellow-sorrel ❀ May–Sept

(Oxalis corniculata) Wood-sorrel Family

- Slender stems grow to 50cm tall
- Yellow flowers with five petals are gathered in slender-stalked clusters
- Leaves are on long slender stalks and divided into three heart-shaped leaflets
- Fruits are stalked, downy capsules

Procumbent Yellow-sorrel is a creeping and ascending perennial weed of roadsides, wasteland and gardens throughout England. This pretty non-native weed is rare or absent from the most of Scotland.

Wall Lettuce   ❀ June–Sept
(Mycelis muralis) Daisy Family

- Branched stems grow to 100cm tall
- Yellow flowers have a ray of five strap-shaped florets and are gathered in loose clusters
- Leaves at base of plant are on winged stalks and deeply lobed, with a larger end lobe. Upper stem leaves are smaller, fewer-lobed and clasp the stem
- Fruits are small black nutlets with a top of white hairs

A perennial herb mainly found on walls and in woodlands in most of Britain, but not in the south-west tip of England or the north of Scotland.

Dandelion   ❀ March–Oct
(Taraxacum officinale) Daisy Family

- Leafless stems grow to 50cm tall
- Solitary yellow flowers consist of rays of strap-shaped florets
- Rosettes of leaves at the base of the plant are cut into opposite pointed lobes, with a larger triangular end lobe
- Fruits are groups of nutlets topped with long white hairs • Wind-pollinated

A perennial of gardens, paths, grassland, dunes and rocky areas. The seeds are grouped together to produce rounded, white fluffy heads. The stems of this plant are often flushed red.

Cat's-ear   ❀ June–Sept
(Hypochoeris radicata) Daisy Family

- Smooth, few-branching stems grow to 40cm
- Flowers are solitary on stems, with rays of strap-shaped florets. Outer florets greyish underneath
- Toothed leaves are hairy, gently lobed and arranged in a rosette around the stem base. Flowering stems have tiny scale-like leaves
- Fruits are one-seeded with white feathery hairs at the top • Insect-pollinated

A perennial herb of dunes, grasslands, meadows and roadsides. Dandelion-like, but has smaller flowers and less fleshy stems. Leaves are edible.

Autumn Hawkbit ❀ June–Oct
(Leontodon autumnalis) Daisy Family

- Few-branched stems grow to 50cm tall
- Solitary yellow flowers consist of rays of florets. The underside of flowers are often streaked red
- Dark green, shiny leaves are cut into opposite lobes with a blunt triangular end lobe
- Fruits are heads of nutlets with a top of feathery hairs • Self- or insect-pollinated

A perennial of grasslands, roadsides, gardens and meadows. This flower is one of the many dandelion look-alikes, and is sometimes hard to distinguish from them.

Mouse-ear Hawkweed ❀ May–Sept
(Pilosella officinarum) Daisy Family

- Hairy leafless flowering stems grow to 25cm
- Yellow flowers consisting of rays of florets are solitary with red streaks on the underside
- Hairy leaves are spoon-shaped, pale underneath and in a rosette at the base of the plant
- Fruits are heads of dark nutlets with a top of white hairs

Mouse-ear Hawkweed is a perennial with creeping leafy stems and is commonly found on wasteland, heaths, grassland, lawns, walls and grassy banks.

Hop Trefoil ❀ June–Sept
(Trifolium campestre) Pea Family

- Grows to 30cm tall
- Yellow flowers are rounded heads of tiny florets that turn brown in fruit
- Stalked leaves are slightly toothed and divided into three oval leaflets
- Fruits are one-seeded pods

Hop Trefoil is a hairy annual of short grassland, roadsides, tracks and sand dunes. It is a low-growing flower, like the Lesser Trefoil, but with more florets held in larger flower heads.

Lesser Trefoil

🏵 May–Sept

(Trifolium dubium) Pea Family

- Grows up to 10cm tall
- Very tiny yellow flowers clustered in round heads up to 7mm across, on slender stalks
- Leaves are stalked and divided into three oval and toothed leaflets. The end leaflet is on a short stalk
- Fruits are one-seeded brown pods, held in heads of remaining flower parts

A small annual of short grassland, roadsides and hedge banks. Similar to Hop Trefoil, but Lesser Trefoil is smaller and has fewer flowers gathered in the heads.

Woodland & Hedgerows

Wild Strawberry
175

Garlic Mustard
175

Woodruff
175

Wind Eyebright
176

Greater Stitchwort 176

Lesser Stitchwort 176

White Campion
177

Ramsons
177

White Dead-nettle 177

Hedge Bindweed 178

Wood-sorrel
178

Snowdrop
178

Wood Anemone 179

Feverfew
179

Gr. Butterfly-orchid 179

Enchanter's-nightshade 180

Cleavers
180

Pignut
180

Cow Parsley
181

Blackberry
181

Hogweed
181

Wild Angelica
182

Common
Valerian 182

Field Bindweed
182

Comm. Spotted-
orchid 183

Dog Rose
183

Butterbur
183

Red Campion
184

Common
Hemp-nettle 184

Cut-leaved
Crane's-bill 184

Rosebay
Willow-herb 185

Broad-leaved
Willow-herb 185

Common Vetch
185

Bush Vetch
186

Common
Mallow 186

Hedge
Woundwort 186

Foxglove
187

Early-purple
Orchid 187

Marsh Thistle
187

Bittersweet
188

Sweet Violet
188

Tufted Vetch
188

Selfheal
189

Field Scabious
189

Bugle
189

Bluebell
190

Germander
Speedwell 190

Field Forget-
me-not 190

WOODLAND & HEDGEROWS

Heath
Speedwell 191

Great Mullein
191

Opposite-leaved
G.-saxifrage 191

Yellow
Pimpernel 192

Marsh-marigold
192

Lesser
Celandine 192

Greater
Celandine 193

Wood Avens
193

Creeping
Cinquefoil 193

Meadow
Vetchling 194

Slender St
John's-wort 194

Perforate St
John's-wort 194

Cowslip
195

Primrose
195

Common
Cow-wheat 195

Common
Toadflax 196

Goldenrod
196

Tansy
196

Smooth
Sow-thistle 197

Nipplewort
197

Wall Lettuce
197

Leafy
Hawkweed 198

Lady's Bedstraw
198

Hedge Mustard
198

Honeysuckle
199

Wood Sage
199

Lords-and-
Ladies 199

Common
Twayblade 200

Ivy
200

Moschatel
200

Common Nettle
201

Broad-leaved
Dock 201

Curled Dock
201

Dog's Mercury
202

Traveller's-joy
202

**Field
Wood-rush** 202

**Bird's-nest
Orchid** 203

**Common
Figwort** 203

Wild Strawberry 🏵 April–July
(Fragaria vesca) Rose Family

- Grows up to 30cm tall
- White flowers have five petals and a yellow centre
- Shiny leaves are on long stalks and divided into three toothed leaflets
- Distinctive fruits are fleshy and red

Wild Strawberry is a creeping perennial herb of dry grasslands, scrub, wasteland and open woodlands. The fruits are instantly recognisable, but are smaller than the variety of strawberry normally found in shops.

Garlic Mustard 🏵 April–June
(Alliaria petiolata) Cabbage Family

- Smooth stems grow to 120cm tall
- Four petalled flowers are grouped in rounded clusters at the top of the stems
- Dark green, toothed leaves are heart-shaped to triangular and are on long stalks lower down the stem
- Fruits are long, curved, slightly angled pods on short stalks • Insect- or self-pollinated

A perennial herb of woodlands, hedgebanks and other shady areas. This plant has a distinctive garlic smell when bruised or crushed underfoot.

Woodruff 🏵 May–June
(Galium odoratum) Bedstraw Family

- Angled flowering stems grow to 30cm tall
- Funnel-shaped flowers have four spreading lobes and are gathered in stalked clusters
- Shiny leaves are in whorls of 6–8 around the stem
- Fruits are tiny with hooked bristles

Sweet Woodruff is a scented perennial herb of damp woodlands, preferring well-drained soils. It is insect-pollinated and has been used as a flavouring for wine.

WOODLAND & HEDGEROWS

Wind Eyebright
(Euphrasia nemorosa) Figwort Family

- Branched stems grow up to 20cm tall
- Tiny white two-lipped flowers have purple streaks and a yellow patch on a lower three-lobed lip
- Dark green leaves often flushed purple are toothed, stalkless and in opposite pairs
- Fruits are small capsules • Insect-pollinated

An annual herb of short grasslands, heaths and open woodland, which has been used in a variety of herbal remedies for eye complaints. Many species of Eyebright grow in Britain, and it is quite difficult to distinguish between them.

Greater Stitchwort ❀ March–July
(Stellaria holostea) Campion Family

- Perennial herb with square slender stems grows to 60cm tall
- White flowers with five petals that are deeply cut to half way down. Flowers are held in loose stalked clusters
- Narrow pointed leaves have rough edges and are in opposite pairs • Fruits are oval capsules

Greater Stitchwort, also known as Star-of-the-Wood, is a wild flower of woodlands and hedgebanks and in the past, as the name may suggest, was thought to cure stitches.

Lesser Stitchwort ❀ May–Aug
(Stellaria graminea) Campion Family

- Grows to 60cm tall
- White flowers with five deeply divided petals, few flowers are gathered in loose stalked clusters
- Small, pointed leaves are narrow, spear-shaped, and are in opposite pairs
- Fruits are round capsules • Insect-pollinated

A hairless perennial herb with slender square stems. It is a wild flower of grassland, hedgebanks, heaths and woodland clearings, preferring acid ground. It is a similar plant to Greater Stitchwort but has smaller flowers, more deeply divided petals and smaller leaves.

WOODLAND & HEDGEROWS

White Campion ❀ May–Oct
(Silene latifolia) Campion Family

- Hairy stems grow up to 100cm tall
- White scented flowers up to 3cm across have five deeply divided petals
- Flowers are on stalks that emerge from where the leaves meet the stem
- Spear-shaped leaves are in opposite pairs with leaves lower down the stem being larger and broader
- Fruits are oval capsules • Insect-pollinated

A hairy annual, occasionally perennial herb of dry arable and cultivated land, wasteland and hedge banks of Britain.

Ramsons ❀ April–June
(Allium ursinum) Lily Family

- Grows to 45cm tall
- White star-shaped flowers are gathered in numbers of up to twenty in rounded heads at the top of the stems
- Up to three long, broad leaves arise from the base of the stem • Fruits are capsules

Ramsons is a hairless perennial herb of damp and shady areas of woodlands and hedgerows and is self-pollinated. The leaves of this plant are edible and have a strong smell (sometimes overpowering) of garlic when crushed.

White Dead-nettle ❀ April–Nov
(Lamium album) Mint Family

- Square stems grow to 60cm tall
- White flowers are two-lipped, open and in whorls around the leafy stems
- Heart-shaped to spear-shaped toothed leaves are in opposite pairs • Insect-pollinated

White Dead-nettle is a hairy perennial of hedgerows, wasteland, roadsides and some gardens. The leaves of this flower are like those of the Stinging Nettle, but do not have the characteristic stinging hairs.

Hedge Bindweed ❀ July–Sept
(Calystegia sepium) Bindweed Family

- Slender creeping stems grow to 300cm long
- Funnel-shaped flowers are white or white with pink stripes
- Alternate leaves are mainly arrow-shaped and are on long slender stalks
- Fruits are one-seeded capsules held in the remaining flower parts • Insect-pollinated

A slender creeping perennial of hedges, hedgebanks, gardens, wasteland and woodland edges. The long entwining stems from which the leaf and flower stalks emerge bleed a white sap when cut.

Wood-sorrel ❀ March–May
(Oxalis acetosella) Wood-sorrel Family

- Slender flowering stalks grow to 20cm tall
- White, solitary flowers have five broad petals with darker veins
- Leaves are on long stalks and divided into three drooping heart-shaped leaflets
- Fruits are angled capsules

Wood-sorrel is a creeping perennial herb of dry deciduous woodland and hedgebanks. In some parts of Ireland this flower is considered to be a shamrock and has been displayed on St Patrick's Day.

Snowdrop ❀ Jan–March
(Galanthus nivalis) Daffodil Family

- Flowering stems grow to 25cm tall
- Nodding white flowers are solitary on stems and have three outer petals and three shorter green-tipped inner petals
- Long narrow leaves all grow from the base of the plant and are keeled
- Fruits are oval capsules

A hairless perennial of woodlands, riverbanks and wasteland, favouring damp areas. The fresh, almost innocent appearance of this flower is deceiving as the whole plant is poisonous.

Wood Anemone
🌸 Feb–May
(Anemone nemorosa) Buttercup Family

- Slender stalks, often flushed red, grow to 30cm
- Star-like flowers have six petals and a pink-purplish tinge on the underside
- Leaves at the base of the plant are on long stalks and divided into 3–5 toothed lobes; leaves on the stem are on shorter stalks and in whorls of three more than half way up the stem

Also known as Windflower, this is a hairless perennial herb with creeping underground stems and is found in woodlands, heaths and moors. It is poisonous, and is a good indicator of ancient woodland.

Feverfew
🌸 July–Sept
(Chrysanthemum parthenium) Daisy Family

- Grows to 60cm tall
- Flowers have a central disc of yellow florets with an outer ray of white florets. Flowers are held in branched, flat-topped clusters
- Light green leaves are cut into bluntly toothed segments; lower stem leaves are on long stalks
- Fruits are hairless, ribbed nutlets

Feverfew is a biennial or perennial herb with branched stems and a strong bitter aroma. It is a wild flower of wasteland, roadsides, hedgerows and gardens.

Greater Butterfly-orchid
🌸 May–July
(Platanthera chlorantha) Orchid Family

- Hairless solitary stems grow to around 50cm
- Scented white flowers with a slight green tinge and a long curved spur are grouped together in loose spikes
- Two broadly oval leaves at base of plant and small, scale-like leaves that grow close to the stem
- Fruits are capsules • Pollinated by moths

A hairless perennial of woodlands, scrub and some grassland on calcareous soils. This wild flower is very like the Lesser Butterfly-orchid, but is taller with larger, slightly darker tinged flowers and a longer flowering spike.

WOODLAND & HEDGEROWS

Enchanter's-nightshade ❀ June–Aug
(Circaea lutetiana) Willowherb Family

- Slightly downy stems grow to 70cm tall
- Tiny white flowers have two divided petals and are gathered in long, leafless spikes
- Stalked leaves are heart-shaped or spear-shaped and in opposite pairs
- Tiny cotton-bud-shaped fruits
- Insect-pollinated

An erect perennial of hedgerows, woodlands and shaded gardens. Animals and people disperse the seeds of this plant as the white, hooked bristles of the fruits easily attach to fur or clothing and are carried away.

Cleavers ❀ June–Sept
(Galium aparine) Bedstraw Family

- Angled stems grow to 150cm long
- Minute, white flowers with four petals are grouped in small clusters
- Leaves, edged with back-turned prickles, are in whorls of between 6 and 8 around the stem
- Tiny, two-celled fruits are covered in back-turned prickles • Insect-pollinated

Also commonly known as Goosegrass, this is a scrambling or climbing annual of hedgebanks, damp woodlands, wasteland and shingle beaches, and also found on arable land.

Pignut ❀ May–June
(Conopodium majus) Carrot Family

- Grows up to 80cm tall
- Tiny flowers have five petals, gathered in domed stalked clusters
- Leaves are divided into feather-like segments towards the base of the plant, and soon wither

Pignut, also known as Earth Nut, is a perennial herb of woodlands, hedge banks and old grassland. The English names of this pretty flower derive from the rounded, underground tuber that was once eaten by foraging pigs.

Cow Parsley
(Anthriscus sylvestris) Carrot Family

❀ April–June

- Grooved hollow stems grow to 150cm tall
- Tiny white flowers have five petals and are gathered in flat-topped to domed umbels
- Fern-like leaves are divided into opposite pairs of pointed leaflets with a similar end leaflet
- Insect-pollinated

Cow Parsley is an erect perennial of rough grassland, hedgerows, woodland edges and roadsides.

Blackberry
(Rubus fruticosus) Rose Family

❀ June–Sept

- Thorny biennial with angled stems growing to 400cm long
- White flowers usually with a pinkish tinge have five petals and many stamens
- Leaves are divided into 3–5 stalked, toothed and oval leaflets
- Fruits are berries that turn black when ripe
- Insect-pollinated

Blackberry, also commonly known as Bramble, can be found in hedgerows, woodlands, scrub, wasteland, gardens and allotments. The distinctive berries of this plant are edible.

Hogweed
(Heracleum sphondylium) Carrot Family

❀ June–Sept

- Grooved stems, sometimes flushed red, grow to 200cm tall
- Tiny white or pinkish flowers are tightly grouped together in umbels up to 25cm across
- Leaves are divided into large deeply lobed and toothed leaflets
- Oval, flat and smooth one-seeded fruits

Hogweed is a large biennial of woodlands, hedgerows, roadsides, streamsides and rough grasslands of Britain. The sap is hazardous: it can burn and blister the skin in sunlight.

Wild Angelica
🌸 June–Sept

(Angelica sylvestris) Carrot Family

- Grooved stems are flushed purple and grow to 200cm tall
- Minute pink or white flowers are gathered in stalked clusters forming dome-shaped heads up to 15cm across
- Leaves are divided into 2–3 pairs of pointed, oval and toothed leaflets, with an end leaflet. There are broad sheaths at the base of the stems

An erect hairless perennial found by streams, rivers, lakes, ditches, wet meadows, marshes and fens preferring more calcareous soils. Has been used to produce a yellow dye as well as a flavouring.

Common Valerian
🌸 June–Aug

(Valeriana officinalis) Valerian Family

- Grooved stems grow to 120cm tall
- Small, scented, pinkish-white flowers with five petals are grouped together at the top of branched stems
- Opposite leaves are divided into pairs of toothed spear-shaped leaflets with a similar end leaflet. Lower stem leaves are stalked.
- Fruits are one-seeded with white hairs at the top
- Insect-pollinated

Common Valerian is a perennial of riversides, fens, marshes and damp woodlands. This plant has been used in the past as a sedative.

Field Bindweed
🌸 June–Sept

(Convolvulus arvensis) Bindweed Family

- Clambering stems grow up to 200cm long
- Funnel-shaped flowers are pink with white stripes, or white or pink stripes
- Green alternate leaves are mostly arrow-shaped and on long stalks
- Fruits are two-celled capsules
- Self- or insect-pollinated

A perennial with creeping underground roots growing well on wasteland, roadsides and some grasslands, and as a weed in arable land and gardens throughout Britain, though quite scarce in the far north of Scotland.

Common Spotted-orchid ❀ June–Aug
(Dactylorhiza fuchsii) Orchid Family

- Smooth solid stems grow to 60cm tall
- Pale pink flowers with short spurs are streaked and dotted purple and gathered in leafy cone-shaped spikes.
- Leaves at the base of the stem are long, broad and covered in purple spots. Stem leaves are smaller and narrower
- Fruits are twisted capsules • Insect-pollinated

A hairless perennial of grassland, scrub, open woodland and hedgebanks. The flowers can also be found in plain white, or white with purple spots and streaks.

Dog Rose
❀ June–July
(Rosa canina) Rose Family

- Prickly stems grow to 300cm long
- Pink flowers have pale centres and five flimsy petals
- Leaves are divided into opposite pairs of toothed, oval leaflets with an end leaflet
- Fruits are fleshy hips

Dog Rose is a prickly shrub of hedgerows, woodland margins and scrub. There are many closely related species that come under the heading of Dog Rose, and most are quite difficult to tell apart.

Butterbur
❀ March–May
(Petasites hybridus) Daisy Family

- Grows to 40cm tall
- Lilac-pink flowers are gathered in stalked spikes
- Leaves are large, toothed, heart-shaped and are on long stalks. The leaves of this plant appear after the flowers

Butterbur is a distinctive perennial with creeping underground stems. It is a plant of wet woodlands, roadsides and wet meadows, and is also found by streams and rivers. Its common name derives from the past use of its leaves to wrap butter.

Red Campion
(Silene dioica) Campion Family

- Grows to 100cm tall
- Flowers are pink with five deeply divided petals, gathered in loose branched clusters
- Leaves are hairy, pointed and are in opposite pairs
- Fruits are capsules with a top of ten teeth

Red Campion is a hairy perennial herb of woodlands, hedgerows and hedge banks. This flower can also be seen in some coastal areas on cliffs and is pollinated by insects.

Common Hemp-nettle
❀ July–Sept
(Galeopsis tetrahit) Mint Family

- Square, hairy stems grow to 100cm tall
- Pink flowers are two-lipped with purplish markings on the lobed lower lip. Flowers arranged in whorls around leafy stems
- Leaves are in opposite pairs, oval and pointed
- Fruits are nutlets held within the remaining flower parts • Self-pollinated

Common Hemp-nettle is a branched, erect annual of arable and cultivated land, hedgerows, woodlands and fens.

Cut-leaved Crane's-bill
❀ May–Aug
(Geranium dissectum) Geranium Family

- Hairy stems grow to around 60cm tall
- Small pink flowers have five notched petals up to 1cm across
- Leaves are divided into lobes that are again divided into narrow segments
- Fruits are hairy, beaked capsules
- Self-pollinated

Cut-leaved Crane's-bill is an annual of grassy places, cultivated and arable land, hedgebanks, wasteland and roadside verges. It is a similar plant to the Dove's-foot Crane's-bill but differs mainly in the leaves.

WOODLAND & HEDGEROWS

Rosebay Willow-herb
🏵 June–Sept
(Chamerion angustifolium)
Willowherb Family

- Grows to 250cm tall
- Each flower has four petals and are grouped at the top of stem to form a loose stalked spike
- Leaves are alternate
- Fruits of this flower are slim capsules

A perennial of woodland clearings and wasteland throughout Britain. It is a great coloniser of dry, open and recently disturbed ground, and was a common sight in London and other bombed cities across Britain during the Second World War.

Broad-leaved Willow-herb
🏵 June–Aug
(Epilobium montanum) Willowherb Family

- Round stems grow to 80cm tall
- Pink to purplish-pink flowers with four notched petals are in loose branched clusters
- Toothed leaves are spear-shaped and in opposite pairs
- Fruits are long downy capsules
- Insect- or self-pollinated

Broad-leaved Willow-herb is a slightly hairy perennial herb of hedgebanks, gardens, walls and woodlands throughout Britain.

Common Vetch
🏵 May–Sept
(Vicia sativa) Pea Family

- Slightly grooved stems grow to 100cm long
- Two-lipped pink or purple flowers are in pairs or solitary along the stem
- Leaves are divided up to eight times into opposite pairs of oblong leaflets that have a tiny bristle at the end. A branched tendril replaces the end leaflet
- Fruits are long flattish pods

A perennial herb that was originally cultivated in Britain as a fodder crop but is now commonly found in meadows, hedgerows, scrub and on the edges of cultivated and arable fields.

Bush Vetch
❀ May–Nov
(Vicia sepium) Pea Family

- Climbing stems grow to 60cm tall
- Pink-purple or blue-purple flowers are two-lipped and gathered in short stalked clusters of up to six
- Leaves are divided into 3–9 pairs of oval leaflets ending in a branched tendril
- Fruits are black hairless pods
- Insect-pollinated

Bush Vetch is a climbing or scrambling perennial of hedgebanks, roadsides, open woodlands and scrub.

Common Mallow
❀ June–Sept
(Malva sylvestris) Mallow Family

- Grows to 100cm tall
- Pinkish-purple flowers with five notched petals and darker veins, in loose short-stalked clusters
- Long-stalked leaves are divided in to 5–7 toothed lobes
- Fruits are flattish, round clusters of edible nutlets
- Insect-pollinated

A low running or erect biennial or perennial with slightly hairy stems, growing on hedgebanks, wasteland and roadsides. The leaves are edible, and infusions from the plant have been made as a remedy for colds.

Hedge Woundwort
❀ June–Sept
(Stachys sylvatica) Mint Family

- Grows to 100cm tall
- Deep pink-purple flowers have white markings on the lower lip and are in whorls around the stem, forming a flowering spike
- Opposite pairs of leaves are oval, pointed, toothed and stalked • Fruits are nutlets

Hedge Woundwort is a hairy perennial with square stems and a distinctive, rather unpleasant odour. It is a flower of woodland, gardens, hedge banks and wasteland and is pollinated by a variety of bees.

Foxglove
❀ June–Sept
(Digitalis purpurea) Foxglove Family

- Grows to 160cm tall
- Pinkish-purple flowers are bell-shaped, with darker flecks surrounded by white markings on the inside of the flower
- Leaves at the base of the stem are broad and stalked, with a wrinkled surface; stem leaves are smaller, narrower and alternate
- Fruits are oval capsules

A downy biennial of open woodlands, hedgerows, wasteland, scrub and roadside verges. The whole of this plant is poisonous but is used to produce a drug that treats heart problems.

Early-purple Orchid
❀ April–June
(Orchis mascula) Orchid Family

- Hairless perennial or biennial growing to 40cm
- Purple-pink flowers are two-lipped with a three-lobed lower lip and purple flecks towards the centre. Flowers are gathered in a short stalked spike
- Leaves are oblong and shiny with dark spots, and all arise from the base of the plant
- Fruits are capsules

Early-purple Orchid is a flower of woodlands, hedgebanks and chalk grassland, and is pollinated by bees.

Marsh Thistle
❀ July–Sept
(Cirsium palustre) Daisy Family

- Hairy, spiny, few branched stems grow to 150cm tall
- Many purple florets emerge from egg-shaped heads that are covered in green-purplish bracts and are gathered in compact leafy clusters at the end of the stem
- Leaves are deeply lobed with spiny edges and hairy above • Insect-pollinated

Marsh Thistle is a biennial of marshes, damp grassland and woodlands. This plant can also have white flowers.

WOODLAND & HEDGEROWS

Bittersweet
(Solanum dulcamara) Nightshade Family

✤ June–Sept

- Scrambling woody stems grow to 200cm tall
- Loose branched purple flowers with five turned-back petals and a cone-shaped cluster of yellow stamens
- Leaves are stalked, pointed-oval, some with two opposite leaflets at the base. Stem leaves are narrower
- Fruits are drooping clusters of bright red oval berries

Bittersweet is a hairy perennial of shingle beaches, woodlands, hedge banks and damp shady areas. The whole of this plant is poisonous.

Sweet Violet
(Viola odorata) Violet Family

✤ Feb–May

- Flowering stems grow to 10cm tall
- Scented, deep violet flowers with five petals are solitary on long stalks
- Heart-shaped leaves are toothed and on long stalks from the base of the plant
- Fruits are capsules

Sweet Violet is a pretty perennial herb of woodlands, hedgebanks and gardens. It is the only scented flower of the violet family and has edible leaves that are rich in vitamins A & C.

Tufted Vetch
(Vicia cracca) Pea Family

✤ June–Aug

- Stems grow to 200cm long
- Purplish-blue flowers are two-lipped and grouped in numbers of up to forty on long-stalked one-sided clusters
- Leaves are divided into opposite pairs of narrow, pointed oval leaflets ending with a branched tendril
- Fruits are hairless brown pods

A creeping or climbing perennial of rough grasslands, scrub, woodland edges and hedgerows.

Selfheal
(Prunella vulgaris) Mint Family
❀ June–Sept

- Grows up to 25cm tall
- Deep bluish-purple flowers are two-lipped and gathered in dense heads with purplish hairy bracts
- Leaves are stalked, oval and are in opposite pairs up the stem
- Insect-pollinated

Selfheal is a perennial herb with creeping stems growing on grasslands, wasteland, lawns and woodland clearings. The common name of this flower derives from its past use to heal wounds and to stop bleeding.

Field Scabious
(Knautia arvensis) Teasel Family
❀ July–Sept

- Slender hairy flowering stems grow to 100cm
- Flowers of bluish-violet florets massed in flat to slightly domed heads
- Leaves are hairy, in opposite pairs on the stem and are deeply divided into pairs of opposite leaflets with an end leaflet; lower leaves are often unlobed, toothed and larger than stem leaves
- Insect-pollinated

A hairy perennial with slender flowering stems growing in open woodlands, grassland, roadsides and hedge banks. This plant has been used in the past to help a variety of skin complaints.

Bugle
(Ajuga reptans) Mint Family
❀ April–July

- Leafy, square, flowering stems with hairs on two opposite sides growing up to 30cm tall
- Blue tubular flowers with white streaks on the three-lobed lower lip are in whorls around the stem and gathered in a leafy spike
- Shiny leaves are stalked and in a rosette at the base of the plant; stem leaves are unstalked and in opposite pairs
- Fruits are black nutlets • Insect-pollinated

Bugle is a perennial herb with creeping stems that can be found in the more shady parts of damp woodlands, wet meadows and hedgerows.

WOODLAND & HEDGEROWS

Bluebell
❀ April–June
(Hyacinthoides non-scriptus) Lily Family

- Smooth, leafless flowering stems grow to 50cm
- Blue bell-shaped flowers with back-turned tips are in drooping one-sided clusters
- Long narrow leaves with a central vein all arise from the base of the plant
- Fruits are oval capsules
- Insect-pollinated

A perennial herb, emerging from underground bulbs, which grows in woodlands, hedgebanks, heaths and moors, preferring lightly shaded areas. This plant is a well-known and easily recognisable flower of spring.

Germander Speedwell
❀ March–July
(Veronica chamaedrys) Figwort Family

- Flushed red stems with hairs on two opposite sides grow up to 30cm tall
- Four-petalled flowers are blue with a white central eye. Flowers are gathered in stalked spikes
- Toothed leaves are broadly oval-triangular and are in opposite pairs
- Fruits are small hairy capsules

A perennial of grassland, roadsides, hedgebanks, woodlands and wasteland. This flower is the most common of the Speedwells found in Britain, and is pollinated by insects or self-pollinated.

Field Forget-me-not
❀ April–Sept
(Myosotis arvensis) Borage Family

- Hairy flowering stems grow to 40cm tall
- Pale blue flowers have five petals and a yellow central eye
- Leaves are hairy and mainly stalkless, with one central vein
- Fruits are nutlets which are held within the remaining flower parts

Field Forget-me-not (or Common Forget-me-not) is a hairy annual of disturbed ground, cultivated and arable land, roadsides and some waste ground.

Heath Speedwell
✿ May–Aug
(Veronica officinalis) Figwort Family

- Hairy stems grow to 25cm tall
- Light blue to lilac flowers have four petals with darker streaks and are gathered in dense, short stalked spikes
- Toothed leaves are oval, hairy and in opposite pairs up the stem
- Fruits are small hairy capsules
- Insect-pollinated

Heath Speedwell is a perennial with creeping underground stems of dry grasslands, open woodlands and heaths.

Great Mullein
✿ June–Aug
(Verbascum thapsus) Figwort Family

- Thick woolly stems grow to 200cm tall
- Yellow flowers with five petals are densely grouped together in a long spike
- Large woolly greyish-green leaves are in a basal rosette, short-stalked, and alternate on the stem
- Fruits are oval capsules
- Self- or insect-pollinated

Great Mullein is a conspicuous biennial of scrub, woodlands, hedge banks and wasteland. The thick hairs of this plant help prevent moisture loss and attacks by insects.

Opposite-leaved Golden-saxifrage
✿ April–July
(Chrysosplenium oppositifolium) Saxifrage Family

- Perennial herb growing to 15cm tall
- Tiny yellow flowers are without petals, and are surrounded by yellowish-green leaf-like structures (bracts)
- Opposite pairs of leaves are rounded, bluntly toothed with a wedge-shaped base
- Fruits are tiny capsules • Self- or insect-pollinated

A plant of wet woodlands, stream sides and wet rocks. Alternate-leaved Golden-saxifrage looks similar but has alternate, kidney-shaped leaves.

WOODLAND & HEDGEROWS

Yellow Pimpernel ✿ May–Sept
(Lysimachia nemorum) Primrose Family

- Grows to 45cm long
- Small yellow flowers have five lobes and are on long slender stalks arising in pairs from where the leaves meet the stem
- Leaves are pointed, oval and in opposite pairs along the stem
- Fruits are capsules

Yellow Pimpernel is a creeping hairless perennial of woodlands and hedgerows, preferring damp shady areas. Creeping Jenny is a similar-looking flower, but has blunt leaves and shorter, thicker flower stalks.

Marsh-marigold ✿ March–June
(Caltha palustris) Buttercup Family

- Hollow, grooved stems grow to 40cm tall
- Yellow flowers with five shiny petals (actually sepals) and many stamens
- Dark green leaves are toothed and heart-shaped. Lower leaves are stalked, with upper leaves clasping the stem
- Seeds are contained in pods
- Insect-pollinated

Also known as Kingcup, this perennial is the large buttercup-like flower of marshes, fens, woodland flushes, streamsides and wet meadows.

Lesser Celandine ✿ Feb–May
(Ranunculus ficaria) Buttercup Family

- Flowering stems grow to 20cm tall
- Bright yellow shiny flowers with up to twelve petals are solitary on long, leafless stems
- Long stalked, dark green leaves are heart-shaped with slightly wavy margins and are all in a basal rosette

A low perennial herb of woodlands, hedgerows and banks of rivers and streams favouring damp areas. Greater Celandine is, surprisingly, not related to the Lesser Celandine and is only similar in that both flowers are yellow and stems exude a sap.

Greater Celandine ✿ May–Sept
(Chelidonium majus) Poppy Family

- Hairy, branched stems grow to 90cm tall
- Yellow flowers with four petals are in small clusters of up to eight at the top of the stems
- Green leaves are divided into opposite pairs of toothed leaflets with a toothed leaflet at the end
- Fruits are hairless, narrow capsules
- Insect-pollinated

Greater Celandine is a perennial herb of wasteland, walls and hedgebanks. The orange sap that emerges when this plant is cut is poisonous and can irritate and stain the skin.

Wood Avens ✿ May–Aug
(Geum urbanum) Rose Family

- Grows to 60cm tall
- Yellow flowers with five petals and many stamens are gathered in loose branched clusters
- Leaves at base of plant are divided into pairs of toothed leaflets, with a larger-lobed end leaflet. Stem leaves are smaller and less divided
- Fruits are heads of hairy nutlets
- Insect- or self-pollinated

A perennial with branching stems, growing in woodlands, hedgerows, scrub and gardens, preferring more shady areas. In the past this pretty flower was thought to ward off evil spirits.

Creeping Cinquefoil ✿ June–Sept
(Potentilla reptans) Rose Family

- Grows to 10cm tall
- Solitary yellow, dish-shaped flowers have five petals and are on long stalks
- Leaves are on long stalks and divided into five seven-toothed leaflets
- Small one-seeded fruits are clustered in round heads • Insect- or self-pollinated

Creeping Cinquefoil is a perennial herb with long creeping stems that are often flushed red. This plant grows well on wasteland, hedge banks, roadsides and dry grasslands.

WOODLAND & HEDGEROWS

Meadow Vetchling 🏵 May–Aug
(Lathyrus pratensis) Pea Family

- Angled stems grow to 120cm tall
- Yellow two-lipped flowers are gathered in long stalked clusters
- Leaves consist of a pair of narrow, spear-shaped leaflets, an end tendril and an opposite pair of arrow-shaped leaf-like structures clasping the stems
- Fruits are pods that turn black when ripe
- Insect-pollinated

A hairless perennial that grows throughout the most of Britain on grasslands, hedgebanks, scrub and woodland borders.

Slender St John's-wort 🏵 June–Aug
(Hypericum pulchrum)
St John's-wort Family

- Slender stems, often flushed red, grow to around 80cm tall
- Yellow flowers have five petals and five sepals with black dots, and are gathered in loose branched clusters
- Stalkless oval leaves are in opposite pairs and covered in translucent dots
- Fruits are three-celled capsules

A hairless perennial of grasslands, heaths and open woodlands and scrubland.

Perforate St John's-wort 🏵 June–Sept
(Hypericum perforatum)
St John's-wort Family

- Grows up to 90cm tall
- Yellow star-shaped flowers have five petals, often with tiny black dots around the edges, and many stamens
- Leaves are oval or oblong covered with translucent dots and in opposite pairs up the stem • Fruits are capsules

Common or Perforate St John's-wort is a hairless perennial of wasteland, open woodland, roadsides, scrub and grassland. Widely used in herbal medicine. The stems bleed a red sap when cut.

WOODLAND & HEDGEROWS

Cowslip   ❀ April–May
(Primula veris) Primrose Family

- Downy perennial herb growing to 10cm tall
- Scented yellow flowers are gathered in stalked nodding clusters at the top of the stem
- Leaves are toothed with a wrinkled surface and are all at the base of the plant
- Fruits are capsules

The Cowslip is a conspicuous flower of open woodland and hedgebanks, as well as some meadows and grasslands. The flowers of this plant have been used in the past as a sedative and to ease nervous dispositions.

Primrose   ❀ Feb and May
(Primula vulgaris) Primrose Family

- Grows up to 40cm tall
- Pale yellow flowers have five notched lobes and a darker yellow centre. Each flower is held on a single leafless stalk
- Wrinkled leaves are tongue- or spoon-shaped and are in a rosette at the base of the plant
- Fruits are capsules • Insect-pollinated

The primrose is a perennial herb that is a familiar site in open woodlands and hedge banks. The whole of this plant has been used for its medicinal properties and is thought to be a particularly good sedative.

Common Cow-wheat   ❀ May–Sept
(Melampyrum pratense) Figwort Family

- Grows to 60cm tall
- Pairs of two-lipped pale yellow flowers arranged in one-sided leafy spikes
- Leaves are in opposite pairs, short-stalked, pointed-oval or spear-shaped
- Fruits are small capsules

Common Cow-wheat is an annual of bogs, woodland clearings and heath land. This plant is partially parasitic, obtaining nutrients from the roots of trees, heather and shrubs.

WOODLAND & HEDGEROWS

Common Toadflax
(*Linaria vulgaris*) Figwort Family ❀ July–Oct

- Grows up to 80cm tall
- Bright yellow flowers are two-lipped with an orange patch on the lower lip and have long straight spurs. Flowers are tightly grouped in spikes
- Narrow leaves are alternate up the stem
- Fruits are oval capsules

Common Toadflax is a perennial of wasteland, hedge banks, cultivated and arable land and some rough grassland. Pollinated by a variety of bees.

Goldenrod
(*Solidago virgaurea*) Daisy Family ❀ July–Sept

- Grows to 100cm tall
- Yellow flowers have both disc and ray florets and are gathered in long leafy spikes
- Leaves at the base of the plant are dark green, stalked and slightly toothed. Stem leaves are narrower, spear-shaped and un-stalked
- Fruits are heads of brown nutlets with a top of hairs • Insect- or self-pollinated

A slightly hairy perennial herb with few-branching stems that grows on dry grassland, heaths, hedgebanks and woodlands. The flowers and leaves can be used to produce a yellow dye.

Tansy
(*Tanacetum vulgare*) Daisy Family ❀ July–Sept

- Grows up to 150cm tall
- Scented flowers are button-shaped, gathered in flat-topped to slightly rounded clusters
- Leaves are toothed and in alternate pairs. Each leaf is deeply cut into opposite lobes with a similar end lobe
- Fruits are nutlets without any hairs
- Insect-pollinated

A hairless perennial herb of wasteland, hedges, roadsides; also found by rivers and streams. Its leaves have been used in a variety of herbal remedies to treat worms, gout and fever.

Smooth Sow-thistle ✿ June–Oct
(Sonchus oleraceus) Daisy Family

- Smooth branched flowering stems grow to 150cm
- Pale yellow flowers consisting of rays of florets are in branched clusters
- Alternate leaves are deeply lobed and sharply toothed; stem leaves clasp the stem
- Fruits are yellow nutlets topped with hairs
- Insect-pollinated

Smooth Sow-thistle is an annual of wasteland, open woodlands and hedgebanks, and is a weed of gardens, cultivated and arable land. In the past this plant has been eaten as a vegetable.

Nipplewort ✿ June–Sept
(Lapsana communis) Daisy Family

- Slender branching stems grow up to 80cm tall
- Yellow flowers consist of a ray of florets and are gathered in loose branched clusters
- Toothed leaves at the base of the plant are stalked, oval with opposite lobes below. Stem leaves are smaller, stalkless and without lobes
- Fruits are hairless, ribbed nutlets
- Insect-pollinated

An annual of hedgerows, wasteland, walls, woodland edges and some gardens throughout Britain. The young leaves of this plant are edible.

Wall Lettuce ✿ June–Sept
(Mycelis muralis) Daisy Family

- Branched stems grow to 100cm tall
- Yellow flowers have a ray of five strap-shaped florets and are gathered in loose clusters
- Leaves at base of plant are on winged stalks and deeply lobed, with a larger end lobe. Upper stem leaves are smaller, fewer-lobed and clasp the stem
- Fruits are small black nutlets with a top of white hairs

A perennial herb mainly found on walls and in woodlands in most of Britain, but not in the south-west tip of England or the north of Scotland.

WOODLAND & HEDGEROWS

Leafy Hawkweed   ❀ June–Oct
(Hieracium umbellatum) Daisy Family

- Branched stems grow to 80cm tall
- Yellow flowers consisting of rays of florets and scale-like bracts that are curved back at the tip. Flowers are in flat-topped clusters
- Stalkless leaves are narrow to spear-shaped, slightly toothed or un-toothed and are mostly alternate
- Fruits are heads of nutlets with a top of white hairs

A hairy perennial of dry grasslands, heaths, roadsides and open woodlands throughout Britain.

Lady's Bedstraw   ❀ July–Sept
(Galium verum) Bedstraw Family

- Square stems grow to 80cm tall
- Scented yellow flowers are tiny with four petals and are clustered along the branched stems
- Leaves are narrow and in whorls of up to twelve around the stem • Insect-pollinated

A perennial herb with creeping stems, growing on sand dunes, coastal heaths and on some grasslands and hedge banks. In the past this flower was commonly used as a stuffing for mattresses and as a flea deterrent.

Hedge Mustard   ❀ May–Sept
(Sisymbrium officinale) Cabbage Family

- Branched stems grow to 100cm tall
- Tiny yellow flowers have four petals and are gathered in short stalked clusters
- Leaves are deeply cut into opposite toothed lobes with a larger end lobe. Stem leaves are smaller than those at the base of the plant
- Fruits are pods that lie close to the stems
- Self-pollinated

An annual or biennial herb of hedge banks, wasteland and roadsides. The plant smells of mustard when disturbed and crushed underfoot.

Honeysuckle

🏵 May–Aug

(Lonicera periclymenum)
Honeysuckle Family

- Leafy stems grow to 600cm long
- Long tubular flowers are pale yellow to orange-yellow with a purplish tinge. Flowers are held in whorls at the end of the stems
- Leaves are oval and in opposite pairs
- Fruits are a small clusters of bright red poisonous berries • Insect-pollinated

A woody scrambling and climbing shrub of hedgerows, woodlands, and walls. The flowers of this plant have a sweet and distinctive scent.

Wood Sage

🏵 June–Sept

(Teucrium scorodonia) Mint Family

- Grows to 60cm tall
- Yellowish-green flowers with only a lower lobed lip are in opposite pairs and grouped in branched spikes
- Toothed leaves have a wrinkled surface, are heart-shaped at the base and in opposite pairs up the stem
- Fruits are nutlets • Insect-pollinated

A downy perennial herb with square stems that are often flushed red. It is a flower of open woodlands, sand dunes, rough grasslands and heaths.

Lords-and-Ladies

🏵 Feb–May

(Arum maculatum) Arum Family

- Hairless perennial grows to 50cm tall
- Flowers of this plant are minute and hidden. Above the flowers is a brownish-purple club-shaped spadix, surrounded by a cream-green cowl-like spathe
- Leaves are arrow-shaped, occasionally with dark spots, at the base of the plant
- Fruits are poisonous red berries that are clustered in a cylindrical spike

An unmistakable flower of woodlands and hedgebanks. This plant has an unpleasant scent which attracts the small flies that pollinate it.

Common Twayblade
(Listera ovata) Orchid Family

❀ May–July

- Grows up to 60cm tall
- Green to yellowish-green flowers have no spurs and are gathered in long spikes
- Leaves are an opposite pair of broad, oval and ribbed leaves towards the base of the stem
- Fruits are twisted capsules
- Insect-pollinated

Common Twayblade is a perennial herb of rough grasslands, open woodlands, scrub and heaths throughout most of Britain, although quite rare in the higher regions of Scotland.

Ivy
(Hedera helix) Ivy Family

❀ Sept to Nov

- Woody climbing stems grow to 500cm long
- Tiny yellowish-green flowers are stalked and gathered in round heads
- Dark green leaves have white veins, are stalked and diamond-shaped or rounded with three to five triangular lobes
- Ripe fruits are round heads of black berries
- Insect-pollinated

A well-known evergreen climber of walls, woodlands, hedgerows and old buildings. The adhesive roots on the stems hold it fast to any object it climbs.

Moschatel
(Adoxa moschatellina) Moschatel Family

❀ April–May

- Stout hairless stems grow to 15cm tall
- Five-petalled green flowers are tightly grouped with four outer facing flowers and one on top
- Long-stalked, pale green leaves are divided into three leaflets, again divided into three segments
- Drooping, fleshy one-seeded fruits
- Insect- or self-pollinated

A perennial of hedgerows and woodlands throughout most of Britain although quite rare in the far north of Scotland. It is also called the 'Town Hall Clock', due to the arrangement of the flowers on top of the stout stems.

Common Nettle
(Urtica dioica) Nettle Family

❀ June–Aug

- Hairy stems grow to 150cm tall
- Tiny green flowers without petals are grouped together in drooping clusters emerging from the base of the leaf stalks
- Stalked leaves are toothed, pointed with a heart-shaped base
- Wind-pollinated

A hairy perennial that grows well in many habitats such as wasteland, woodlands, hedge banks, roadsides and fens, and by rivers and streams. Both the stem and leaves are covered in stinging hairs that irritate the skin on contact.

Broad-leaved Dock
(Rumex obtusifolius) Dock Family

❀ May–Oct

- Grooved stems grow to 130cm tall
- Tiny green flowers with a red tinge are in whorls around the stem
- Large, heart-shaped leaves; upper stem leaves are smaller and narrower
- Fruits are tiny triangular nutlets
- Wind-pollinated

A hairless perennial herb of hedgebanks, wasteland, cultivated and arable land and by the sides of rivers and streams. This plant is a thriving weed with leaves that are renowned to ease the rash of nettle stings.

Curled Dock
(Rumex crispus) Dock Family

❀ June–Oct

- Slightly grooved stems grow to 120cm tall
- Tiny green flowers are sometimes flushed red and gathered in large numbers around the stems in long spikes
- Long spear-shaped leaves are green, untoothed with crumpled margins
- Fruits are one-seeded in the papery remains of the flower parts • Wind-pollinated

A hairless annual, biennial or perennial of wasteland, roadsides, hedge banks, cultivated and arable land and some coastal areas such as shingle beaches.

WOODLAND & HEDGEROWS

Dog's Mercury

🌸 Feb–May

(Mercurialis perennis) Spurge Family

- Creeping, hairy perennial growing to 50cm tall
- Flowers are tiny and green, with male flowers held in spikes and female flowers in clusters of up to three
- Toothed leaves are pointed, oval and in opposite pairs
- Fruits are hairy capsules

A poisonous plant of deciduous woodlands and hedgerows. The male and female flowers are held on separate plants, and are wind-pollinated.

Traveller's-joy

🌸 July–Sept

(Clematis vitalba) Buttercup Family

- Woody stems grow to 10m long
- Flowers have four greenish-cream sepals with many stamens and are gathered in branched, stalked clusters
- Leaves are divided into opposite pairs of toothed and stalked leaflets with a similar end leaflet
- Fruits are nutlets with long feathery hairs

A climbing shrub of woodland margin, roadside verges, hedgerows and wire fences, preferring chalk and limestone soils. Also known as Old Man's Beard.

Field Wood-rush

🌸 March–June

(Luzula campestris) Rush Family

- Brownish stems grow to 25cm tall
- Tiny brown flowers with yellow stamens are gathered in dense clusters
- Grass-like leaves are mainly at the base of the stem, and are covered in white hairs
- Fruits are brown oval capsules

Field Wood-rush is a tufted perennial of grasslands and gardens throughout Britain.

WOODLAND & HEDGEROWS

Bird's-nest Orchid ❀ May–July
(Neottia nidus-avis) Orchid Family

- Brown stout stems grow to 40cm tall
- Pale brown flowers have no spur and are gathered in spikes
- Leaves are pale brown and scale-like
- Fruits are twisted capsules
- Self- or insect-pollinated

Bird's-nest Orchid is a chlorophyll-free perennial of shaded woodlands, particularly beech woodlands, and is usually found amongst deep leaf-litter where this plant gains all its food to survive. The name of this plant derives from the tangled nest-like structure of its roots.

Common Figwort ❀ June–Sept
(Scrophularia nodosa) Figwort Family

- Grows to around 80cm tall
- Tiny flowers with a purplish-brown upper lip and green lower lip are in long-stalked, branched clusters
- Short-stalked leaves are toothed and in opposite pairs
- Fruits are oval capsules
- Insect-pollinated, particularly by wasps

A distinctive perennial with square stems growing in woodlands and hedgerows, preferring damp areas. The tubers of this flower are edible (not recommended, as they don't taste very good).

WOODLAND & HEDGEROWS

Glossary

ALIEN: Flowers that were introduced into Britain, and have since naturalised

ANNUAL: Flowers that complete their lifecycle within one year

ANTHER: Part of the stamen containing pollen seeds

ARABLE: land suitable for crop production

BIENNIAL: Flowers that complete their lifecycle within two years

BRACTS: Often leaf-like structures found close to the flowers or on the flowering stalks

BULBIL: Small bulb that usually develops in a leaf axis or on the flowering part of the stem

CALCAREOUS: Soil and ground containing calcium carbonate

CALYX: Collective term for the sepals of a flower

CAPSULE: A dry fruit that opens to release its seed when ripe

COWL: Hood-shaped covering surrounding the flower part

DECIDUOUS: Group of trees that shed their leaves each year or periodically

EVERGREEN: Group of trees that retain their leaves throughout the year

FLORET: Small flowers that are grouped to form a flower head

HEATH: Poor, acid, well-drained land that is dominated by dwarf shrubs

HERB: A non-woody plant that has been or can be used for culinary or medicinal purposes or as a scent

KEEL: Leaves of a flower that are folded lengthwise like the keel of a boat

NODULES: For the purpose of this text nodules are rounded lumps on the roots of plants

NUTLET: A small, dry, one-seeded fruit

PERENNIAL: A plant that can live for several years, usually flowering every year

RHIZOME: Underground root-like stem with both roots and shoots

ROSETTE: A rose-like cluster of leaves

SEPALS: Usually a green outer ring of floral leaves that surrounds the flower

SPATHE: A leaf-like structure that surrounds the flower cluster

SPIKE: A flower cluster formed closely or on short stalks on a long stem

STAMEN: The male reproductive organ of a flower

TENDRILS: Slender, climbing structures usually found at the end of the leaf

TUBER: A thick rounded part of a stem or underground stem

UMBEL: A flower cluster in which stalks spring from a common centre and form a flat or curved surface

WHORL: A ring of leaves around a stem of a plant

WOODLAND FLUSHES: Where a stream runs through a wood

Index

Index (continued)